'The power of our voice – as an integral part of not just what we do, but who we are – comes across throughout this informative and thought-provoking book. Starting from an investigation of sound production and the purpose of vocal sound as a powerful tool for communication, the reader is compelled to think differently about their own voice; to become more self-aware of how it is used and how it could be developed to better effect. For a teacher, this critical self-analysis of the power of our own voice is a key to effective delivery across the multitude of situations in which our varied work takes us. Its applied approach, weaving together a strong theoretical underpinning with a series of practical exercises, will be of benefit to any teacher wanting to reflect upon and develop their work and enhance their wellbeing.'

Dr Alison Daubney, Senior Teaching Fellow,
University of Sussex, UK

'This is an important and wide-ranging book that covers not only the use and protection of the voice, which is important for teachers as a topic in its own right, but also the ways in which teachers use their voices as key mechanisms for pedagogy. But in addition to this it also covers important areas relating to the different ways in which teachers actually find their own teaching voices, and what sorts of voice are appropriate on various occasions. These areas alone would make this book worthwhile, but what makes this book really stand out is that it also deals with the under-researched area of beginning teachers setting out to *find* their own voices. This is a fascinating and worth-while subject area, and is so important in the early professional lives of all educators. This important book has something for all those who work with children and young people, and will make an important addition to the staff library of all schools and colleges.'

Professor Martin Fautley, Director of Research in Education,
Birmingham City University, UK

Using Your Voice Effectively in the Classroom

As a teacher, you are required to use your voice more than any other professional! Your voice is the most important tool that you have at your disposal to inspire students and help them learn effectively. Using your voice powerfully and successfully is the key to becoming an outstanding teacher. Developing a strong vocal presence in the classroom influences everything else that you do, helping to build your confidence and positive interactions with students. If you neglect your voice as a teacher, you are more likely to end up stressed, have a shorter teaching career and suffer from vocal health issues.

This book explores how you can learn to use your voice effectively in the classroom, linking together basic theory about vocal production and teacher identity with numerous practical tips, tricks and exercises that you can apply to your own teaching. Covering all aspects of the voice and its employment inside the classroom as well as its importance to daily life outside, the book tackles topics such as:

- the philosophy of the voice, how it develops and its role in creating your own identity

- the mechanical and mental skills required to develop a teaching voice

- acquiring confidence and an exploration of body language to underpin your vocal production

- the relationship between the student's voice and the teacher's voice

- the importance of practice for a teacher

- the practicality of caring for one's voice.

Using Your Voice Effectively in the Classroom offers a much-needed exploration and thorough examination of the voice in the classroom and will be an indispensable guide for trainee teachers, as well as valuable reading for all practising teachers.

William Evans is Senior Lecturer in Education at the Faculty of Education, Manchester Metropolitan University, UK.

Jonathan Savage is Reader in Education at the Faculty of Education, Manchester Metropolitan University, UK. He is also Managing Director of UCan Play.

Using Your Voice Effectively in the Classroom

William Evans and Jonathan Savage

 Routledge
Taylor & Francis Group

LONDON AND NEW YORK

First published 2018
by Routledge
2 Park Square, Milton Park, Abingdon, Oxon OX14 4RN

and by Routledge
711 Third Avenue, New York, NY 10017

Routledge is an imprint of the Taylor & Francis Group, an informa business

British Library Cataloguing in Publication Data
A catalogue record for this book is available from the British Library

Library of Congress Cataloging in Publication Data
A catalog record for this book has been requested

ISBN: 978-1-138-64978-1 (hbk)
ISBN: 978-1-138-64979-8 (pbk)
ISBN: 978-1-315-62571-3 (ebk)

Typeset in News Gothic
by Florence Production Ltd, Stoodleigh, Devon

Contents

Introduction

Welcome to this book on your voice! We hope you enjoy reading it as much as we have enjoyed writing it. Over the last 18 years, we have worked with thousands of teachers and helped them develop their teaching in primary and secondary schools across the United Kingdom. We have observed teachers working in a diverse range of schools from independent schools in leafy parts of Cheshire, to inner-city comprehensives in south Manchester. There is one thing that all these teachers have in common, something that they all use every day as part of their teaching – yes, you've guessed it – their voice! However, despite the voice being an integral part of 99.9 per cent of every teacher's arsenal of 'tools', there has been very little published literature about the teaching voice and how this can developed. Hence this book! Welcome!

But (we can hear sceptical voices already), why the need for this book? Surely, they might say, your voice is your voice? You've got what you've been given and you just use it as it is? Why bother trying to 'reinvent' something that is as natural and intrinsic to ourselves as our voice for an activity like teaching?

Well, there are numerous answers to this question and several of these will be explored throughout the book. For now, let's just say that a cornerstone of our argument here is that your natural voice, i.e. the one that you have had since birth, is perhaps not the same as what will become your 'teaching' voice. Clearly, the two are going to be closely linked but one will be quite distinct from the other in all kinds of ways. We hope that this is not such a surprising or alarming assertion? After all, you no doubt already have a range of 'voices' that you might use within different contexts or with different people. Certainly, a 'parental' voice might have a different tone, character and inflection to the voice that you might use with a partner or close friend; the voice you adopt on a formal occasion like a job interview is going to be very different from the one that you might utilise within an informal social occasion. What you say, and how you say it, changes in light of these contextual factors.

One other key reason for us writing this book, which we might as well get out in the open right at the outset, is that we have been alarmed by the number of teaching friends and acquaintances that have suffered from vocal health problems over the years. This often seems to strike teachers in the middle part of their careers and can lead to all kinds of further stresses and strains and, in the worst cases, early retirement. As we have explored the research in this area, we have found that this is not a problem limited to the United Kingdom and its schools. It is something that afflicts teachers worldwide. On the basis that prevention is better than cure, we wanted to write a book that helped you, as a young teacher, to learn to care for your voice and nurture it in such a way that it will help you enjoy a long and happy teaching career.

So, throughout the book we'll be considering how your voice is integral to becoming a skilful teacher. We'll be looking at how your voice functions, and how it can be used as productive tool to help facilitate teaching and learning; we'll also be considering how what you say, as well as how you say it, can impact on your teaching. Furthermore, and most importantly perhaps, 'finding your voice' is far more than just developing your vocal delivery as a teacher. It is about embarking on a journey of developing your own understanding of what makes you 'you'! Once commenced, it challenges your own perception of what constitutes your teaching identity and, from this, a whole new pedagogical style can flow.

How did your voice end up where it is today?

Harari (2011) argues in his book *Sapiens* that somewhere between 70,000 and 30,000 years ago the brain of Homo sapiens changed. His theory of change and the 'tree of knowledge' (Harari 2011, p. 22) gives us a starting point in our journey exploring our voices. In his narrative exploring how humans inhabited the earth, a recurring theme is that language has governed much of our ability to develop individually and relate to one another.

Early hunter-gatherer tribes would have needed to communicate to survive much as many animals still do today. Anyone who has a dog will know this simple truth. Will's dog, an over confident miniature dachshund, constantly reminds him of his alertness to killer-postmen or annoying people who dare to walk past his living room window! His brain (the dog's, that is) is working overtime to keep himself and his pack alive and he is able to communicate this to Will quite clearly. He has yet to find the necessity to sit and chat with Will about these dangers and how they might seek to lead a calmer, 'bark free' life.

In the broader evolutionary context, it would be logical to consider that early human communication would have been much the same, the drive for survival being the main controlling factor. It is clear looking back though that we didn't decide, or evolve, to stay as small groups of Homo sapiens wandering the earth hunting and gathering food each day. As humans evolved, they began to settle and live in larger groups, perhaps principally for safety and other mutual benefits. As these groups became larger, communication becomes ever more complex and important. Human brains evolved rapidly within this context and in ways that other mammals did not. What holds back large groups of monkeys from forming together increasingly larger groups and moving very quickly to the top of the food chain is certainly not their physical ability (individually, humans would be no match for this) but perhaps their inability to communicate in more complex ways.

So, voice, communication and language have been key to our development as humans for many thousands of years. But what is so special about our language?

Let's start by dismissing a few reasons as to why it is not that special! It was not the first language. Every animal has some kind of language. Even insects, such as bees and ants, know how to communicate in sophisticated ways, informing one another of the whereabouts of food. Neither was it the first vocal language. Many animals, including all ape and monkey species, have vocal language. For example, green monkeys use calls of various kinds to communicate. Zoologists have identified one call that means 'Careful! An eagle!' A slightly different call warns 'Careful! A lion!' (ibid., p. 24).

So, if our language was just about communicating and surviving, it seems that it could be argued that there is nothing particularly special about it. Even if we extend our consideration to more complex sounds these can also be seen (and heard) in other animals such as whales and elephants. Many common birds have the ability to mimic our language, copying every sound but this again is not special or real communication. However, what is quickly apparent is that Homo sapiens developed language systems that are considerably more complicated in their range of sound and meaning than other species. As Harari puts it:

> The most common answer is that our language is amazingly supple. We can connect a limited number of sounds and signs to produce an infinite number of sentences, each with a distinct meaning.
>
> (ibid.)

Our language and communication evolved to not only help us to survive but also to help us communicate complex and interesting ideas. Over time, we have evolved in our abilities to share these imbued with meaning and nuance. Amongst a huge variety of things, it has enabled us to share fantasy lands, abstract ideas and build shared belief systems.

This leads to Harari's second theory about our communication, that our language evolved to enable us to talk about us.

> ... the most important information that needed to be conveyed was about humans, not about lions and bison. Our language evolved as a way of gossiping. According to this theory [we] are primarily a social animal. Social cooperation is our key to survival and reproduction. It is not enough for individual men and women to know the whereabouts of lions and bisons [thus to survive and behave

like monkeys]. It's much more important for them to know who in their band hates whom, who is sleeping with whom, who is honest and who is a cheat.

(ibid., pp. 25–26)

As our ability to communicate developed it is clear that so did our ability to be even more social. We developed the ability to live in larger groups, to communicate, to gossip, to tell ever more complex stories to each other.

The human voice developed as the principal form of communication within these larger groups. Most theorists seem to think that song, or pitched communication, would have come before complex language. It is a much more simple step from warning noises to incantations to raise the spirits of early man or to entertain a small group of hunter-gatherers than it is to the complex language we use to communicate today.

But what is crucial to this book, to yourself, to humans, is that your voice is of unique importance to you to support communication. It is not the only way we can or do communicate, but those that use it and use it well need to know more about it.

Evidence of early singing, group worship and man moving to believing in the unknown or fictional is clear but is difficult to measure or trace with clarity. Luckily, for us (or the authors), this is neither important nor crucial. What is clear looking from our modern vantage point is that it did happen and communication, even global communication, is one of the most important parts of our modern world. Perhaps one of the most argued worries of modern communication is the loss of the human voice within it. We are uniquely connected yet not connected at all, we are all 'alone together' (Turkle 2011).

What part language played in the movement of man from reasonably far down the food chain to the top of it is difficult to imagine or prove exactly. But it is clear that language, voice and communication are a key part of what separates us from all other species. It is a key part of what makes us human, of what makes us who and what we are. We will be applying some of these theories in the opening chapter when we build a theory of the voice within the context of your own identity.

In Chapter 1 we will think about your journey so far and how episodes in your own development will have profoundly affected how you think about and hear your own voice. It will tackle the principle that the use of voice is a deeply personal thing and will challenge you about this physically and conceptually. The chapter will give practical advice on how to make sense of your journey so far and from this plan a voyage of discovery for your own teaching voice.

Chapter 2 will explore the mechanical, physical and mental skills needed to develop the teaching voice. It will draw on research and work with experienced singers and actors to exemplify key approaches. Everyone has a voice to develop, and although some will find this easier to develop than others, you can improve your vocal delivery through simple, carefully structured exercise. Specifically, the chapter will consider the basics of breathing, air flow, air speed, production and how you can better understand how you can make a broad range of vocal sound.

Chapter 3 starts from the premise that if you are the most interesting thing in the room, pupils will listen to every word you say! Your voice is their most obvious form of communication. From it, your pedagogical approach is enhanced or limited. This chapter will seek to develop ideas of how the voice links more closely to your pedagogy, and how development of both is inextricably linked. Being more skilled, enthusiastic and confident with your voice will allow you to develop your pedagogy in new and innovative ways. More importantly, the inner confidence that will come from understanding and being confident with your voice will allow you to think differently about your teaching.

Following on from the pedagogical theme of Chapter 3, Chapter 4 will explore how your voice is explicitly linked to your body language work within the classroom. Key teaching scenarios will be explored to demonstrate how an effective teaching voice works in conjunction with your body language to create a strong teaching identity. This has many applications. One of the most common applications will be to help you create a clear behaviour management strategy that is positive and affirming and not negative and confrontational.

In the same way as one's voice shapes one's teaching, teaching shapes your voice. Giving pupils confidence to understand their own voices, both literally and meta-phorically, will help to empower their work, their thinking and learning. It is too easy to presume that because your voice comes so naturally you understand how to use it and develop it. This does not happen automatically. In Chapter 5 we will explore the links between the teacher and student voice and how each informs and mediates the other. It will draw on research into varying education cultures and methodologies, which place student voice at differing points. We will consider how your work as a teacher can help or hinder long-term development. This chapter will link to principles of learning, and consider how pupils really learn within a broad context mediated by your own and their voices.

Chapter 6 will draw together the practical principles of the previous chapters and consider them alongside the work of Matthew Syed that challenges theories associated with talent and practice. This chapter will dispel some popular myths about 'talent' and explain in clear and concise ways how practice is key in developing all one does as a teacher. It will consider how this practice can be built into your daily work so that it is an integrated part of everything you do. Furthermore, it will briefly consider the inner challenges we all face as humans, teachers and professionals to have strong, confident and stress-free careers. In line with the key principles explored in the previous chapters, it will demonstrate how vocal confidence is key to your personal and profes-sional development.

Chapter 7 takes a more metaphorical look at the voice. It will explore a range of metaphors around the voice, e.g. the 'inner chimp' and 'chimp paradox' drawn from sport and performing arts. It will develop some of the basic themes explored in previous chapters and reinforce the key message of the book that one's voice is a clear view into oneself, as a person and teacher, and how one thinks and operates. We will demonstrate how one's voice links to how one thinks as an teacher, how this confidence and understanding controls one's development, planning and one's interactions with the fast-paced responsiveness that is needed to work effectively within the classroom.

Finally, looking after one's voice is a key part of all vocal development. Sadly, too many teachers soon find that their voice is strained, damaged and a worn-out tool. In the final chapter we will consider how you can complete the daily act of teaching, communicating and practice without damaging the voice as an instrument. We will also help you unpick bad habits in order to promote better methods and ways of working with your voice.

References

Harari, Y. N. (2011) *Sapiens: A brief history of humankind.* London: Penguin.
Turkle, S. (2011) *Alone Together.* New York: Basic Books.

Chapter 1

Finding your voice

ICONIC VOICE PORTRAITS

Karen Carpenter is popularly rated as one of the best female vocalists of all time. The music of the Carpenters and the continued success of her brother, Richard, in writing and producing others in the music industry, reflects that they had abilities that were far greater than just Karen's voice. But what was so unique about Karen's voice?

It is clear when you listen to her sing, and I encourage you to do this now, that her voice has a natural appeal. It draws you in, not only by her story-telling ability but in its pureness of quality and tone. Having spent my lifetime submerged in music I have had her voice cited as one that many wish to copy on their instruments, not just singers. So, without being too technical, what is it about her voice?

Pitch – it is said that she had a large vocal range, something like four octaves. This, even if unverified, is a little unusual. You can certainly hear a good range that she uses in various songs. What is so surprising is that she uses the lower part of her voice far more than the upper register. Certainly, in many of the songs, her singing starts with this very characteristic low sound. Listen to a few songs, just the start of her vocal. Notice how she starts low in pitch, the songs often build in the middle section or the chorus but there was something very distinct about her voice in this range, which allows you to know it's her within just a few seconds. Her voice is not as recognisable in the upper part of its register. A great example of this is the opening of *Yesterday Once More*. She certainly uses the chest part of her voice, or the lower sound to give it a distinct characteristic.

Air – without getting too technical, Karen is a master of putting through lots of air in her voice. To get a visualisation of this in your mind imagine that the air from her lungs, supported by her diaphragm, is travelling down a piece of pipe to her vocal chords where the sound is produced. If the pipe had a small diameter, it wouldn't have much air going to the voice. Karen sings as though this is a wide pipe, with lots of air going to the voice. You can hear this in how 'big' but not loud the voice sounds. This isn't just a trick of the musical engineer or excellent practice in the musical group. She is supporting her voice with lots of air. Thus, it has a depth, size and quality that flows over us like honey tipping slowly from a jar. It is viscous, thick and luxurious in quality. Karen also supports this by pushing the air slowly. She rarely gets too loud. You can further tell that she is pushing the air slowly by her ability to sustain and sing long phrases. She also keeps the lyrics supported. There are few gaps in the lyric line. Even though the words are so very clear, compare that to many modern singers; you can rarely hear a moment where the sound isn't sustaining.

Her voice is interesting – there are so many things that could be cited as why she is so interesting. The first two points already support this but her ability to tell the story of the song with subtle inflections, the range of timbre she uses and smooth delivery draw us in. You want to listen. I would be surprised if you went to a music streaming site to listen to her voice that you only listened to one song. There's something about her voice, not just the music, that makes you want to hear more. Listen to how she makes her voice interesting. It is rare that she stays for long at one volume, at one timbre or sound; listen to how she accents different parts of words. Listen to how well the voice is supported by air and how clearly she articulates the words. You could write down the lyrics to every song, easily.

Lastly, she does all of this by developing and embracing her 'natural sound'. I don't know what vocal training Karen had or how much she thought about how she sung but it certainly sounds so natural. Of course, the problem with this is that anyone who's great at something seems natural; it seems easy, but what we should take from this is that we all have a natural sound at this point. We must all embrace this first, to begin to develop.

To help in understanding this voice I would also encourage contrasting it against other female singers. Try to consider how they use pitch, air and how they try to be 'interesting'.

Suggested listening: Beyonce, Katy Perry or Sia.

> Of all the tools for cultural and pedagogical intervention in human development
> and learning, talk is the most pervasive in its use and powerful in its possibilities.
>
> (Alexander 2008, p. 92)

Let's start this chapter with a question. Do teachers talk more or less today than they
did 40 years ago? And perhaps a follow up question, would it be better if they spoke
more or less today?

The answers to these questions are hard to ascertain but they are interesting to
consider. Why not ask some of your older friends and relatives about teachers that
taught them and the role of 'talk' within their pedagogy? Perhaps a common view is
that in previous generations teachers did talk more than they do today. Current teaching
theory tends to place a lower value on long periods of teacher talk, arguing that it can
lead to student disengagement. Rather, proponents might argue, it is important to
develop a mixed economy of interactions in the classroom, where individual work,
paired or group activities, student feedback, self and peer assessment, all have a part
to play alongside the 'limited' monologic of extended periods of teacher talk.

However, this view has not always held sway. A broader reading of the educational
literature can easily find examples of teachers from previous generations whose teaching
style differs immensely from those considered fashionable today but were nonetheless
undoubtedly effective at the time. One of the most powerful examples is recounted by
Professor Robin Alexander in his book on pedagogy (ibid.) where he recounts the story
of his English teacher at the Perse School in Cambridge during the 1950s and 1960s.
We would encourage you to read Chapter 7 in this book in its entirety, but here is a
paragraph from the opening where Alexander introduces the style of teaching that he
experienced and the role of 'talk' specifically in the pedagogy of Douglas Brown:

> Talk was hugely important to him, and I have met few talkers as fluent or as
> undemonstratively eloquent, but in today's classrooms he would be counted
> somewhat monologic. Yet, not once in my recollection did he take the easy route
> of recitation teaching, the ritualised default mode of classroom interaction, for he
> saw learning as enquiry and advocacy rather than simple transmission, and in
> that spirit his questions were utterly authentic.
>
> (ibid, p. 156)

So, talking per se is obviously not the problem. Talk done well can be inspiring and
engaging; talk done solely for the transmission of knowledge ('recitation' in Alexander's
words) is a poor substitute for a richer pedagogical approach. He continues:

> In any case, he had no need of the safety net that recitation affords for those
> teachers whose limited knowledge of what they teach confines them to the
> security of test or recall questions, beyond which they stray at their peril. Instead,
> his forte was kind of two-layered exposition: telling and explaining, but also and
> especially *showing* [his italics]. That is to say, letting the words and music that

were his passion themselves do the work, having sensitised us to their power and inducted us in ways that this power might be unlocked.

(ibid.)

This paragraph stresses the importance of your subject knowledge. Having a deep knowledge of your subject or subjects gives you the platform from which deep and meaningful talk can spring. Alexander is rightly critical of teachers whose subject knowledge relies solely on the information needed to help students pass an examination or do well in a class test. For him, and for his English teacher Douglas Brown, 'telling and explaining' was only the beginning of authentic teacher talk; 'showing', by which he means a much deeper form of communication that blends words with ideas and meaning inextricably linked to the subject at hand, was the most powerful form of classroom discourse.

This subject link is worth pursuing a little further. As well as teaching English, Douglas Brown was an accomplished musician and shared his passion for music with students at the school. This was done with considerable aplomb. Alexander's reflection on his teacher concludes with the following moving paragraph:

With Douglas, moreover, there was not one teacher but four: language, literature, music and the man through whom the power of these was unlocked. Not for him the self-important strutting of those teachers whose authority resides in position rather than talent, and whose educational vocabulary neither liberates nor ignites but instead fawns on the clichéd eduspeak of the latest government initiative. He knew, and he wanted us to know, that the words and music mattered much more than he, and in this he displayed the humility of genius and the artistry of teaching at their best.

(ibid., pp. 171–172)

Subjects matter. Of course they do. But who we are as teachers matters more. Are we going to be the one who is able to unlock the joy of learning about language, literature, music, chemistry, geography or whatever your subject expertise is, within the lives of our students? Training students to pass an examination is important. But a true education goes wildly further than that and who we are, what we say and how we say it really matters in achieving these loftier goals.

Should teachers talk in classrooms? Yes! They should talk well. Do teachers talk more or less in classrooms today than 40 years ago? Our answer is probably less (due to range of reasons) but there are strong arguments for them to talk more providing that the 'type' of talk is one that promotes engaging and meaningful learning through an empowering dialogue with students.

The richness of the narrative around talk in work by educational theorists like Robin Alexander stands in stark contrast to the frameworks that inform the processes by which teachers obtain their qualified teacher status. Documents such as the Teachers'

Standards (DfE 2017) make no mention of the type of quality of teacher talk that might be expected in the work of a qualified teacher. Similarly, the documentation that Ofsted produce in relation to school inspection makes no mention of the requirement for teachers to demonstrate an ability to talk well. This does seem strange given the role that talking plays in human development. It is interesting that we hear a lot about student voice in many educational publications; the teacher voice is (often) strangely absent.

This chapter will help you think about your journey so far and how episodes in your own development will have profoundly affected how they see and hear your own voice. It will tackle the principle that the use of voice is a deeply personal thing linked explicitly to your broader identity. From this, your teaching identity, including your teacher voice, will emerge.

Where does your teaching identity come from?

> Good teaching cannot be reduced to technique; good teaching comes from the identity and integrity of the teacher.
>
> (Palmer 1998, p. 10)

As we have discussed in the opening to this chapter, your voice is one part of what makes your whole teaching identity! Although your voice is the main focus of this book, we felt it was important to start by considering your teaching identity as a whole, before narrowing down the focus onto your voice itself.

The process of learning to teach is an exciting one. It contains challenges of various types – intellectual, practical, physical and emotional. It will be unlike anything else you have ever done. But there will be important things that you have done in your life that you can draw on to help you become a teacher. Whilst this may be true in a practical sense (i.e. you may have been able to establish and maintain good, professional relationships with young people through helping out at a local youth club), it is also true in a psychological sense. The person that you are today has been formed through a mixture of your genetic disposition and your life experiences, relationships and activities. These have shaped your personality, your speech, body language and ways of thinking and acting. Teaching is a new type of mental and physical activity. But 'you' are going to do! Every part of you will be challenged by it and, if you are doing it properly, it will be demanding. So, we hope that you are prepared!

Developing your sense of identity as a teacher is the theme for this opening chapter of the book. As authors and academics involved in delivering courses of initial teacher education, this is a deliberate choice. We firmly believe that as you seek to develop a broader understanding of where you have come from as a person, relate and apply this to your new, emerging role as a teacher, and complete the reflective cycle by reflecting on the teaching you are undertaking, then the chances of you becoming a skilful and effective teacher will be increased. The extracts that we have chosen to assist us in this process all identify different areas related to identity, teaching and reflection that will help you begin to get to grips with developing your teacher identity.

Palmer's article (Palmer 1998) is a useful exposition of this chapter's key theme. Good teaching is firmly based in the identity of the teacher. But what does that really mean? How can I begin to understand my 'identity' and use that knowledge to help ensure that my teaching is really built upon a firm foundation?

Our dictionary gives a range of definitions for the term 'identity'. These include:

- The collective aspect of the set of characteristics by which a thing is definitively recognisable or known;

- The set of behavioural or personal characteristics by which an individual is recognisable as a member of a group;

- The quality or condition of being the same as something else;

- The distinct personality of an individual regarded as a persisting entity; individuality.

There are a number of important, basic points to note here. First, identity is about something being known or recognised. For our discussion, it is what makes you the person you are (physically, emotionally, intellectually, spiritually, etc.). It may also be elements or characteristics that other people can recognise in you.

Second, identity is often linked to a relationship. An object's identity may be related to or distinct from another object within a particular group. The particular aspects of your identity are best understood when one contextualises them in different ways (e.g. your actions in a particular context could be seen as being representative or demonstrative of a specific element of your identity, which can be perceived by others and, therefore, mark you out as a particular individual). This is particularly important when you seek to develop a new identity for a new type of activity (e.g. teaching). The contextualisation of aspects of your 'pre-teaching' identity within the new activity of teaching that you are undertaking will be an important aspect of your reflective practice in the process of your early initial teacher education.

Seeking to understand who we are and how what we are translates into the new role of teacher is not necessarily an easy journey. We have helped many students along this voyage of discovery through our work running PGCE courses at Manchester Metropolitan University. On some occasions, at the beginning of our course in September we are met by confident students who have already completed significant periods of teaching in schools or other educational settings. They have discovered their teaching identity through these experiences and are able to build on this throughout their academic studies. For others, the journey can be a little more prolonged and challenging. As tutors, we are often faced with having to address key points in relation to their body language, facial expressions, temperament, inter and intra-personal skills as well as aspects of their voice and vocal delivery. These can be challenging conversations as they go to the very heart of who we are as people. By raising sensitive issues of this type we are challenging who that person is as well as what their teaching identity 'looks' like, not only from our perspective as tutors but also, importantly, from the perspective of the young people being taught.

The key point here is that your teaching identity builds on the raw materials of who you are. But it will probably end up being a different 'version' of who you are because of the formal context within which you are working. Thankfully, few teachers, in our experience, would behave the same in the classroom as they would in the pub on a Friday evening! But, to put it another way, our teaching identity will be structured around the key components of who we are as a human being. Every teacher is unique because every human being is unique. As we often say to our students, teaching is not a science; it is an art built around a human relationship between ourselves as teachers and our students.

So, it is important to have a framework by which you can analyse your identity. A core part of this relates to the key ways of thinking or knowing that make you the individual that you are. Peshkin defines this as our 'subjectivity' (Peshkin 1988, p. 17). His work highlights the requirement for us to be 'meaningfully attentive' (ibid.) to this subjectivity as we conduct our daily lives and the teaching activities that they contain. We would also argue that at key moments of transition, e.g. the process of initial teacher education, these things are especially important.

Peshkin describes subjectivity as a 'garment that cannot be removed', which has the capability to 'filter, skew, shape, block, transform, construe, and misconstrue' what we are and how we act (ibid.). In other words, in order to truly understand what it means to be a teacher we must first attempt to understand ourselves. He refers to it as a 'veil' through which our view of ourselves (and the world) is mediated. The impact of this veil on our sight cannot be removed but we can seek to understand its effect and learn to see differently on occasions. Cheater puts it like this:

> We cannot rid ourselves of our subjectivity, nor should we wish to; but we ought, perhaps, to pay it very much more attention.
>
> (Cheater 1987, p. 172)

Although Peshkin would not have called himself a school teacher, his research goes onto to helpfully demonstrate this process through the identification of subjective 'I's that he perceived and reflected on during an extended piece of educational research at Riverview High School in California. He observed the education that the school offered its students over a number of years, even moving his family home into the school's catchment area for the duration of his stay. You can read more about this study in his book, *The Color of Strangers, the Color of Friends* (Peshkin 1991). It is a superb example of a naturalistic study of education, with disturbing conclusions for issues around race and ethnicity.

There are number of important introductory points here. Firstly, the foundations for Peshkin's subjective 'I's are drawn from a range of sources, including

- His own belief and value systems;

- His experiences of a particular environment, i.e. the town of 'Riverview';

- His ongoing experiences of life within the particular school;

- The wider community and the relationships that he, and other members of his family, established within that community.

Secondly, Peshkin categorises his subjective 'I's in two main ways:

1. 'Intrinsic Subjectivities' that make up his whole reflective 'being', i.e. they are context-less (at least in basic ways, e.g. geographically) and remain the same wherever he is or whatever he is doing;

2. 'Situational Subjectivities' (Peshkin 1988, p. 18) that change from place to place, i.e. they are contextualised in some way.

The following two case studies show how Peshkin's intrinsic and situational 'I's can be applied in the development of one teacher. Following each case study, a series of activities designed to help you conduct a similar piece of reflective work will be presented.

CASE STUDY 1
DEFINING INTRINSIC 'I'S (FROM SAVAGE 2011)

Through a piece of structured reflection, I have identified the following intrinsic subjective 'I's that I believe have been an important influence on my work. They are presented chronologically, although you will quickly see that there are many overlapping, competing and conflicting dimensions.

1. The Musically Conservative 'I'

This is, in a sense, the easiest 'I' for me to identify. It has existed for the longest and runs back in my memory to early childhood. It has its foundation in my training as a musician in the classical tradition, as a pianist from the age of five and a percussionist from the age of 11. The strict disciplines of instrumental learning and performance practice are clearly etched in my memory alongside the immense enjoyment of being part of an orchestral group giving public performances. I grew up to love the music of the Western classical tradition and, in many senses as a teenager, to despise the music of popular traditions.

continued

2. The Musically Radical 'I'

My Musicological-Radical 'I' was more difficult to identify. Strange as it seems now, this 'I' seemed to have developed, to an extent, alongside the Musically Conservative 'I' in my later teens. I remember an eccentric woodwind teacher at my sixth form college introducing my colleagues and me to a range of contemporary classical music. At first, I did not understand the strange sounds that this music contained, but over the course of two years my musical palette began to broaden. This continued as a number of my friends began to compose experimental music of various types. As a percussionist, I was often called upon to perform these pieces and grew to love a broader palette of sound sources and textures.

But, like many performers, I was never that keen to engage in the act of composition itself. In contrast to my performing career, I had no formal tuition in composition beyond the stylistic pastiche exercises of Bach chorales and two-part inventions at Advanced level. It was only as my piano playing developed alongside my interest in jazz that I began to learn to improvise and compose within this idiom. Ironically, the knowledge of music gained via my Musically Conservative 'I' put me in a strong position to learn about and understand the harmonic and melodic features of jazz.

3. The Pedagogically Inclusive 'I'

My experience taught me that there was only one way to learn about music. This was an exclusive and elitist activity available only to those that had sophisticated performance abilities and an understanding and appreciation of the Western Classical tradition. But at some point, which I find it hard to put my finger on, I realised that there had to be another way into music that was less exclusive and elitist. This did not happen as a result of my own teacher training experience. In the gap between this last sentence and the previous one I have spent over an hour reading through my old assignments and teaching practice materials from my PGCE studies. I can hardly find any references in them to any significant discussion, argument or belief statements that signal a change in my attitude from presenting an approach to musical study that was any different from the kind that I myself experienced and succeeded in. There is one exception to this bleak picture that will be described below.

I believe that the development of my Pedagogically Inclusive 'I' is tied up intricately with the establishment of the Technological-Enthusiast 'I'.

4. The Technological-Enthusiast 'I'

As a high school pupil I remember shying away from computers and seeking to adopt more traditional approaches to working with pen, paper, manuscript paper

continued

and conventional instruments. The strength of my Musically Conservative 'I' meant that I had strong views about the types of music that I preferred and led me to disparage popular music and the ways in which it was produced. However, when I left music college in 1989 my brother gave me his old computer and I began to use it to record pieces of music. A friend and I fancied ourselves as songwriters and we made and recorded tracks with other vocalists. I used my musical notation skills to write arrangements for various people including the covers band that I played keyboards in.

It was as a young teacher at my first school that I began to appreciate the importance that technology could play in widening access to music for a different type of pupil than myself. My experiences of using technology had always been to reinforce and consolidate my musical practices in light of my Musically Conservative 'I'. My Musically Radical 'I' had been nurtured and fed through my undergraduate studies and, to a degree, through my PGCE. My Technological-Enthusiast 'I' spoke to me strongly during my early years of teaching and out of this melting-pot I believe that my Pedagogically Inclusive 'I' was born. Music education must be for all and not a few. I wanted to research and find ways to achieve this.

5. The Artistically Appeasing 'I'

Through a lecture given during my PGCE course by a community musician, my view of what counted as 'artistic practice' was challenged at a fundamental level. Rather than focus solely on artistic objects, he asked us to value the processes by which these objects were formed as well as the experiences contained within these processes. In many ways my career to this point had been about faithfully recreating artistic objects for others to enjoy and little attention had been paid to enjoying the process of making or recreating those objects. Yet, I think that here are the seeds of my belief as a teacher that musical process is as important as musical product for our children. This cuts right against everything that I was taught and valued for many years. My musicality was judged against performance outcomes and I succeeded as a musician because my musical 'products' were considered acceptable.

This is why I have called this final subjective 'I' my Artistically Appeasing 'I'. My dictionary gives three definitions for the word 'appease':

1. To bring to a state of peace or quiet.

2. To cause to subside.

3. To pacify or conciliate, especially: to buy off (an aggressor) by concessions usually at the sacrifice of principles.

continued

Whether within the classroom environment or the lecture theatre, I feel that I am appeasing many elements of my Musically Conservative 'I', bringing them to a state of peace or quiet. But this is not in the sense of buying off or giving concessions. There have been no concessions given or principles sacrificed. My Artistically Appeasing 'I' believes deeply in the genuine artistic practice of young people's classroom work at a philosophical, aesthetic and educational level. The ideals and beliefs of the Musically Conservative 'I' are still present. I still love the music of the Western Classical tradition and have sought to pass on that passion to my pupils in various ways. But I believe that the process by which these convictions have been appeased and, in a sense, broadened has made my approach to teaching more inclusive and tolerant of the various pathways by which pupils can come to know and understand musical knowledge and develop personal ways of expression.

PRACTICAL TASK

Spend some time trying to analyse your own intrinsic 'I's. You can do this in a number of ways. This is a highly personal exercise. Reflect on the key notions or concepts that underpin your beliefs about teaching and learning. Think through:

- Underpinning beliefs or philosophies (beyond the educational) about your subject and the impact it has had on your life throughout your childhood and formative years;

- Your own educational experiences and memories through formal and informal contexts (i.e. school, university but also the home, local community, etc.);

- Conversations (or recollections of conversations) with key people that you have met who may have changed the way you think or feel about your subject;

- Your reading and the powerful ideas that this might have contained that might have impacted you personally or educationally;

- Family or other relationships and how these may have shaped your personality and affected your teaching ability;

- 'Eureka' moments from your own life experiences.

> There will undoubtedly be all kinds of other sources for your ideas here too.
>
> Labelling your intrinsic 'I's is difficult but important. Try to get down to the base level here and ensure that each 'I' has a distinctive 'flavour' or 'personality'. Putting ideas into categories can help with this process. Try and end up with four or five intrinsic 'I's of your own. This will help you in the next stage of the exercise.

For Peshkin, intrinsic 'I's are the dominant voices within ourselves. By undertaking the practical task, we hope that you have been able to think differently about key aspects of your own subjectivity.

Moving onwards, Peshkin's argument is that these intrinsic 'I's come into play at key moments of innovation or change within our personal or professional lives. For us, this could relate to the key topic of this book – helping you find and develop an effective voice for the classroom.

As an example, the following case study explores how the intrinsic 'I's identified in Case Study 1 came into play at a particular moment in this teacher's career. At this particular point, the teacher was about to undertake a piece of educational research within his teaching. Through this consideration of intrinsic 'I's in practice, it was possible to define a range of 'situational "I"s'. These, in turn, related closely to a specific series of choices about the educational activities to include within the piece of research.

CASE STUDY 2
DEFINING SITUATIONAL 'I'S (FROM SAVAGE 2011)

1. The Facilitative-Curriculum 'I'

At a very early stage in my career I began to realise that the curriculum was more than a written document or statement of learning objectives and outcomes. Within my initial teacher training I was taught to plan lessons and schemes of work with thought and consideration, specifying key learning objectives, choosing appropriate teaching activities and identifying possible outcomes by which I might know that my pupils have learnt something. The strict nature of this teaching model fell well within the realm of my Musically Conservative 'I'. It was built on the belief that I could determine the pathways and processes of musical development for my pupils. I knew what was best for them, or so I thought, and

continued

I could plan for a range of teaching activities that would bring these supposed qualities out. What worked for me in my musical development would work for them in theirs. But even at the time of my training this all felt very deterministic and slightly at odds with what I considered was a key defining feature of artistic practice – namely unpredictable pathways of working and diverse musical outcomes.

This dilemma was exacerbated by my Technological-Enthusiast 'I' that sought to consider the educational implications of moving technologies out of the music studio and into the music classroom. This was uncertain ground for me and required a new approach to curriculum planning and delivery.

The result of this conflict was the Facilitative-Curriculum 'I' that grew throughout my PhD studies. In its early development it was nurtured and given credence by my reading of work by Stenhouse and others. Stenhouse's vision of the classroom and the curriculum as opportunities for cultural development inspired me to think about and plan for a music curriculum, facilitated through ICT, that truly gave space for pupils to develop and learn about the 'culture of music' in ways that matched what I conceived to be authentic musical and artistic processes.

One particular question posed by Stenhouse became very important as I planned for these early studies of musical learning and teaching with new technologies:

> The problem of the curriculum can now be expressed as follows: what worthwhile curriculum content can we find as a focus for a classroom experience which will stimulate the pupils to an attempt to find for themselves standards which are worthwhile and viable in terms of their own experience of life?
>
> (Stenhouse 1975, p. 133)

This question challenged head on my conception of the curriculum as a closed spiral of 'creative' possibility managed and controlled by the teacher. Pre-determined outcomes to an artistic problem, however helpfully presented by myself to the pupils, were second rate when compared with Stenhouse's vision of classrooms as 'cultural laboratories':

> The classroom becomes a kind of cultural laboratory in which new face-to-face culture is generated at a humble level. The pupils are in fact not making a transition from one culture to another, but rather being provided with the opportunity to feed their own culture on the arts and sciences, and thus to build for themselves an enriched medium of communication

continued

and thinking. . . . The teacher ought to be a servant of his (sic) pupils, asking himself how his subject can make a contribution to the quality of their living.

(Stenhouse 1975, p. 134)

I saw the establishment of a facilitative and empowering curriculum as one key ingredient in trying to create a classroom culture within which pupils could begin to make creative connections. I also realised that from the pupil's perspective the curriculum became embodied in my role as their teacher. I cannot remember any occasions when pupils asked to see my lesson plans. For my pupils, my own musical values, understanding and practice was what mattered.

The development of this Facilitative-Curriculum 'I' began to solve what I can now perceive as a conflict between my Musically Conservative 'I' and Pedagogically Inclusive 'I'. My ability to redefine the curriculum as a facilitating environment for musical exploration and discovery through the careful use of ICT (as demanded by my Technological-Enthusiast 'I') was central in this process.

2. The Embodied-Curriculum 'I'

Linked to the Facilitative-Curriculum 'I' is the Embodied-Curriculum 'I'. Whilst I sought to consider and plan projects that prioritised opportunities for pupils to re-imagine and enrich their musical thinking through the imaginative use of ICT, I quickly became aware that the quality of my relationship with my pupils was the most important ingredient in seeking to cultivate what I perceived as authentic musical practices with ICT. I had to learn to value pupils and place their experience of the curriculum centre stage in my thinking. To do this meant taking my focus away from the written or planned curriculum to a certain extent and placing it firmly on charting pupils' lived experiences of the curriculum, representing this in as authentic a way as possible through my written evaluations.

I describe this as the Embodied-Curriculum 'I'. As such, it reflects my desire to allow pupils to experience music at a deeper, more personal level than I experienced through my Musically Conservative' 'I'. It draws on aspects of my Musically Radical 'I' which saw, at that impressionable age of my mid-teens, that music was as much an embodied experience as a subject to be analysed and studied from afar. Similarly, it draws on my Artistically Appeasing 'I', which has taught me that the process of being involved in music can be as intrinsically valuable as the final product of that music making. I still believe that high quality musical products are highly motivational for pupils and that they have an important part to play in their education. But as pupils begin to appreciate and

continued

embody curriculum processes their attention shifts from final product to an enjoyment of the activity of music making for its own sake. This is a long journey for me to undertake, and one that I am still engaged in. However, at whatever stage in the journey I was constantly aware that the influence of my Embodied-Curriculum 'I' was central to my teaching and research process.

3. The Democratic-Compositional 'I'

Where does my belief in composition as a dominant force in music education come from? This question has puzzled me throughout my research. It is not that composition has played a large part in my own music education. I would not describe myself as a composer and, in many ways, would be uncomfortable about any public audition of my work. For me, composition has essentially been a private thing. So, apart from a requirement in the National Curriculum to teach composition, why overtly stress the importance of composition and use it as a central practice throughout my research?

I have thought long and hard about this. I believe it comes down to a strong dissatisfaction with my own experience of music education that was privileged, elitist and, as discussed above, built entirely around notions of instrumental ability and performance skill. Many other pupils who I knew were not offered the same experiences and opportunities as I was. They grew to dislike music lessons and to see them as an irrelevance. But, as is the case with the majority of young people, music played a huge part in their wider lives. I succeeded through this model of music education but many others failed. This did not bother me at the time but it does now. There has to be another approach.

I believe that through the prioritising of composition I have provided a more democratic music education for my own pupils. My Technological-Enthusiast 'I' spotted an opportunity for change. At the start of the research process I was tentative about this. My Musically Conservative 'I' was a strong force and I was tempted to fall back on personal experiences of music education that had worked for me. However, with the ongoing observation of other composers' work, and the support of key individuals, I was able to pursue and develop an alternative model of music education that had a focus elsewhere. Did this new prioritising of composition in my work provide a field of equal opportunities for pupils? Probably not, but it is a lot more level than it was before. I believe that my Technological-Enthusiast 'I' has been justified through the development of the situational Democratic-Compositional 'I'. More pupils have been able to succeed in this model of music education than did through the one that I experienced as a child.

Peshkin's concept of intrinsic and situational subjectivities ('I's) provides a lens through which one can generate a more holistic view of oneself, one's beliefs and core values and how they might impact on one's teaching. Your 'subjective "I"s' will change and develop over time, but it is important to remember that Peshkin's core belief was that your 'intrinsic "I"s' are developed and shaped very early and are carried through your life and applied within the various locations, activities and roles that you find yourself in or undertake.

We can illustrate this easily, and we will do this in two main ways here.

First, whether you are working within a primary or a secondary school, many of you will have a particular subject area that you have been trained to teach. Goodson writes that:

> School subjects provide a context where antecedent structures collide with contemporary action; the school subject provides an obvious manifestation of historical legacies with which contemporary actors have to work.
>
> (Goodson 1991, p. 118)

If you are working in a secondary school, the subject-based culture that you work within is underpinned by a significant historical legacy. This can lead to fundamental differences of opinion about what should be taught within a particular subject, how it should be taught and assessed. The same is true, perhaps to a lesser extent, within the primary school where subject boundaries are less rigid but knowledge is still compartmentalised within strategies for literacy and numeracy, or within thematic or topic based curriculum approaches. You may also be in the position of having responsibility for a particular subject area of the primary curriculum. Jephcote and Davies give a flavour of the complexity of the situation by picking up on Goodson's notion of the 'teacher as actor'; someone who has to work within different contexts or levels in order to present the subject as a meaningful 'whole' within the curriculum:

> Changing the curriculum is an outcome of contexts between actors in different arenas and at different levels. Its story needs to be told at a number of levels to reflect the membership and structure of subject communities and to provide a means of illustrating each level and their interconnectedness. At the micro-level accounts have been concerned mainly with teachers, school classrooms and subjects and at macro-level with processes of policy-making and its implementation. At the same time, the meso-level has been taken to comprise of subject associations, local education authorities and sponsored curriculum projects where there are mediating processes which provide means to reinterpret macro-level changes and to assess the range of new choices they present to subject factions.
>
> (Jephcote & Davies 2007, p. 208)

? REFLECTIVE TASK

Unpicking these subject subjectivities or cultures and relating them to one's own intrinsic and situational subjectivities is an important extension of Peshkin's subjective and situational 'I's. Key questions to ask at this point would include:

- What are the subjectivities that underpin an individual subject? How can these be defined and articulated?

- How do these relate to the teacher's own, declared, subjectivities about their role and purpose as an educator?

Second, and moving beyond individual subjects and their specific areas of knowledge and forms of understanding, within classrooms we can note that there are various different forms of interaction between teachers and students that will demand different forms of action (including different forms of speech). Drawing on research done by Alexander across a number of European countries (Alexander 2008, p. 109, these include:

1. Whole class teaching through which the teacher is required to relate to the whole class simultaneously (not an easy gig!), individual students are to relate to their teacher and also to each other collectively;

2. Collective group work, in which the group work is led by the teacher (so can most easily be conceived as a scaled down form of whole class teaching);

3. Collaborative group work in which the teacher sets a task and students then work on the task independently for the most part with interventions from the teacher when required;

4. One-to-one activity through which the teacher works with individual students; and,

5. One-to-one activity in which students work together in pairs.

Your subjectivities, that 'veil' through which you seek to understand the world as you see it (in Peshkin's terms) comes to play here in a similar way to that in which you seek to understand specific subjects and their contribution to your own and your students' learning. When you are seeking to plan a sequence of learning, to what extent are your choices about the form of the learning opportunities you want to include prejudiced by your own subjectivity? Can you seek to neutralise this? Would you want to?

In summary then, there are powerful forces at work in your teaching identity. Your genetic makeup, your upbringing, your own experiences of education, friendship and love, knowledge, skill and understanding are all integral to who you are as a person. It is from this rich milieu that your teaching identify is formed. It will be like you, but not completely you; it is a partial, more public facing, version of you that you will have to learn to love whilst recognising that it is, by its nature, slightly contrived. In our view, there is certainly an element of acting in good teaching. But it is just an element. There is a very good strong dose of authentic humanity in every great teacher and recognising that in yourself is a key part of your journey in developing your own, authentic teaching identity.

It is from these experiences that your teaching voice will develop. As we will go onto see in Chapter 2, what your teaching voice actually sounds like and how you go onto use it will take you on another equally interesting journey of discovery.

We began our chapter with a description of the iconic voice of Karen Carpenter. For those of us of a certain age we only have to hear a note or two of her voice to recognise her unique vocal sound. Of course, the sadness was that her life had a darker side to it, one less public and full of pain and struggles. It is hard to listen to her songs without hearing some of that angst in her voice on occasions. Alongside the great technical ability that she had, the raw human emotion in her voice transcends many of the more transient musical elements and styles that her recordings represent. There is something timeless in them that is hard to describe.

For our discussion, we need to remember that what you will sound like as a teacher is something that is intensely personal. Our voices are shaped over decades and their imprint is unique. We've noticed recently that some telephone banking systems have vocal imprints as part of their security systems! We will not be asking you to change your voice in order to become an effective teacher. This would be as difficult (and silly) as us asking you to change your personality or your 'subjectivities' in Peshkin's terms. Rather, we will be asking you to examine and understand your voice in a new way, and seek to develop it further within the specific context that teaching demands in your school. Core elements will remain. Other elements will change depending on who you are teaching, where you are teaching them, and how you are seeking to go about it. Your voice is a powerful tool. It is the most powerful tool you have at your disposal. We will try and help you to use it well.

References

Alexander, R. (2008) *Essays on Pedagogy.* London: Routledge.

Cheater, A. P. (1987) 'The anthropologist as citizen: The diffracted self'. In Jackson, A. (ed.) *Anthropologist at Home*. London: Tavistock.

DfE (2017) 'Teachers' standards'. https://www.gov.uk/government/publications/teachers-standards [last accessed 21/3/17].

Goodson, I. F. (1991) 'History, context and qualitative methods'. In Goodson, I. F. & Walker, R. (eds) *Biography, Identity and Sociology.* Basingstoke: The Falmer Press.

Jephcote, M. & Davies, B. (2007) 'School subjects, subject communities and curriculum change: The social construction of economics in the school curriculum'. *Cambridge Journal of Education* 37:2, 207–227.

Palmer, P. (1998) *The Courage to Teach: Exploring the inner landscape of a teacher's life*. San Francisco, CA: Jossey-Bass Inc. Publishers.

Peshkin, A. (1988) 'In search of subjectivity – one's own'. *Educational Researcher* 17:7, 17–22.

Peshkin, A. (1991) *The Color of Strangers, the Color of Friends: The play of ethnicity in school and community*. Chicago, II: University of Chicago Press.

Savage, J. (2011) *Cross Curricular Teaching and Learning in the Secondary School*. London: Routledge.

Stenhouse, L. (1975) *An Introduction to Curriculum Research and Development*. London: Heinemann Educational.

Chapter 2

Developing your voice

ICONIC VOICE PORTRAITS

Morgan Freeman has an iconic voice. Instantly recognisable, within the films he has worked he has portrayed God and the President of the United States of America (these are not the same, despite what the current occupant of the oval office might say!), narrated the presidential campaigns for Hillary Clinton and Barack Obama, and you can even have him narrating your journey as part of a new satellite navigation system app!

Freeman's voice is one of extremes. It can be mesmerizingly calm and soothing, yet it can also be angry and forceful. These kinds of extremes take a lot of vocal expertise and skill, something that Freeman himself puts down to an excellent vocal coach and training programme that he undertook whilst at drama school. The underlying rich, full, gentle tone is probably the key feature that we remember from his voice.

In analysing Freeman's voice, many commentators have picked up on its low, resonant tone linked to some of the dominant, strong, male role models that he has played throughout his acting career. In one experiment, Casey Klofstad at the University of Miami recorded men and women saying the phrase 'I urge you to vote for me this November' and then digitally raised and lowered the pitch of the recordings before playing them to members of the public. Both men and women voted for the deeper versions of the voices from both the male and female recordings. Why? We have an inbuilt disposition to trust lower-voiced individuals who we perceive to have greater integrity, competence and physical power.

Freeman, for his part, has his own theories about the power of voices like his. 'If you're looking to improve the sound of your voice, yawn a lot', he once said in an interview. 'It relaxes your throat muscles. It relaxes your vocal chords. And as soon as they relax, the tone drops. The lower your voice is, the better you sound' (Oaklander 2016).

This chapter will explore the mechanical, physical and mental skills needed to develop your teaching voice. As we considered in the previous chapter, your teaching voice is a key part of your teaching identity, which, in turn, builds on the key 'subjectivities' that make you the person that you are. Throughout the chapter, we will continue to consider a range of educational research, whilst also building on work we have done with experienced singers and actors to exemplify key approaches through which you can build an effective teaching voice. Everyone has a voice to develop, and although some will find this easier to develop than others, our contention is that we can all improve our vocal delivery with positive effects in our classrooms. Specifically, this chapter will consider the basics of breathing, air flow, air speed, production and how you can better understand how you can make a broader range of vocal sound.

CASE STUDY

We are all born singers. It is just at some point in your life you are often told that you can't sing. I was in Year 4 at primary school when it all happened for me (although at this time I'm not sure it was called Year 4; those details escape me slightly).

Choir practice was conducted at lunchtimes and we often had extra rehearsals in school time when a performance or show was imminent. On the whole I liked our music teacher. I spent much time in music and my friends all played instruments. This is why I started playing an instrument, although I never got a choice of which one, it was just what was left. Going to choir seemed a natural extension of this and I got involved. On this particular day as we practised along the teacher spotted something that wasn't 'in key' or on the tune. She kept us singing. Wandering across the front of the choir listening for the problem, she sought to identity the child who couldn't sing, the one who was ruining it for everyone else! She got closer and closer to the section where I was standing in the second row. As she did, something inside me said, 'It's you, she's coming for you'. Instantly, I began to sing quieter. She continued past, scanning back and forth a few more times. The moment passed and we all moved on and sang another piece. I never did find out if it was me that was the offender, but something inside me said it was. I slowly started to miss choir and eventually I didn't go anymore. The moment had arrived for me. I wasn't even ten years old and already I knew, I couldn't sing.

Since his experiences in the Year 4 choir, Will's musical career has flourished. He is an expert tuba player and plays with one of the world's leading brass bands. But throughout his career in teaching, this story has come back to his mind many times.

The choir teacher here (who we are all now secretly hating!) wasn't trying to single out Will or anyone else; they were trying to do the best for all the pupils and choir in general. At least this teacher was taking time to run the choir, supporting their students' music education and giving up their free time. But, this teacher had ruined Will's singing career before it had even got started. He lost his confidence to sing, to have a go, to be involved.

Sadly, this is a story with which many of us are familiar. Our first experiences of singing within school are often not positive ones. More generally, the first 'rules' that children encounter in school relate to sitting quietly and being still. This is seen as a 'good' thing to do, whereas singing and dancing around is seen has being silly or, worse, characterised as bad behaviour.

Prior to attending school, the formative environment of the family home can also provide a contrasting and interesting insight into how vocal production is nurtured and encouraged. As parents, we can remember the faltering moments of our children's vocal development and how this developed with interaction from family members, friends and others. Parents are often overjoyed by the first sounds that their children make. The joys of Facebook and other social media are a modern testament to this (*puts down computer, picks up phone to watch a plethora of videos of toddlers copying words, accidentally swearing and other jollities accompanied by unbridled support and pride from onlooking videoing parents! OK, back to work . . .).

Within the family home, things that accompany children's early vocalisations are shared joy, support and encouragement. We are encouraged to produce phonemes (all 44 of them we learnt recently) and turn these gurgles, sounds and phonemes into words without formal teaching. Child listen and copy, learning their first language quickly over their early years by modelling these vocalisations on the words, phrases and sentences they hear from their parents and siblings. We have never seen a parent stopping a child from talking because they said 'hopitell' instead of 'hospital', or 'bassgetti' instead of 'spaghetti'. In fact, it is supported, enjoyed and reinforced. Correction often comes in just repeating words back with the 'correct' pronunciation or just joining in knowing that the 'correct' words will eventually come out.

As infants, our first interactions with our own vocal 'sounds' are often joyful because they are supported and celebrated by all. As babies turn into toddlers they increasingly move from individual play to shared play, mixing with peers and learning the skills of cooperation and sharing. The primary form of communication is their language and, again, we have never heard youngsters correcting each other for the sake of a correction! They use their natural language to communicate and play. At this age, developing their voices is a natural process and a key part of their wider physical, psychological and sociological development. It happens in line with our evolutionary disposition to communicate together, to play with others, and to bond together. We practise with our voice, we copy 'experts', turning their sounds into our language and as we do we adapt and modulate it with our own interpretations, experiments and improvisations.

Children do this without fear and with total confidence. As Wooten says, 'they do it with freedom'. (As an aside, we would encourage you to watch Victor Wooten's TED video, 'Music as a Language'. It will at least give you a break from reading!)

There are many ways to consider your own vocal development. We would encourage you to take a few moments now to note down how you feel about your voice. Was your communication and vocal development encouraged and supported as a youngster? Do you have positive or negative stories about how your voice was used within a school environment, whether that be for singing or something else?

REFLECTIVE TASK

Write down three short memories of using your voice, talking, communicating, whilst you were young, let's say before you left secondary school. After writing these three short extracts down use this as data to critically evaluate what this instilled in you. Did it positively support your vocal development or introduce or support a problem or worry. Did you have a 'nice', strong or confident voice? Or had you developed worries about your voice, its sound, or vocal delivery? How were these exposed and have you been supported in seeking to respond positively to any worries about your voice in any given context?

If we go back to Will's initial story, he can begin to understand his vocal development as a youngster. Certainly, his loss of confidence was key. This would stop him attending choir rehearsals until much later in my life, after he had become an accomplished instrumentalist. But, he always approached this with caution, singing just below the volume of others, avoiding solos or even leaving sections out. As regards to his voice in other situations, it had the opposite effect. Looking back, he over compensated with his personality and voice to make sure he was a leader in classroom and social situations, often speaking too loudly rather than too quietly!

Since those days, Will and Jonathan have had their own children (seven between us) and we have seen that youngsters do start with confidence in their voices. They experiment with their own sound; they are happy with it, whatever it is, and they use it to communicate with others and sing quite naturally.

As a second reflective task, consider how singing is perceived or practised within your own life. There are cultures, societies and religions that seem to place more importance on singing as a form of community, communication and place in the family. History also tells us that there were times when singing was more central to our daily lives. But consider this for yourself. Where you live, your background, your work context, and even your age, may shape your opinions on and thoughts about the use of your voice.

REFLECTIVE TASK

Consider the area in which you live, the society, community and school and importance that is put upon singing or developing vocal confidence within this context. What are the key factors here? After you have made a list, consider which of these you have no, some or total control of.

For most primary school students, one of the first rules that they learn at school is to be quiet. Whilst also quickly helping you to learn what you are not very good at (sadly), schools convince children that being quiet is a virtue. Sitting quietly is also quickly confused with listening, something we often say to our student teachers, but that's getting a little off the point.

So, for many children in school their journey begins by them being encouraged to lose their voices. They learn to sit quietly, trying to focus on their teachers, communicating with others in a very set manner by raising their hands and only speaking when being spoken to. What is the result of this? Anecdotally, it seems that few pupils leave primary school with the vocal confidence to talk in front of a large group of peers and parents.

What would schools look or sound like if more was done with children to support their vocal delivery and confidence? What would this do for us as confident orators in later life? How would this shape our vocal development and our social and personal development at this time?

Developing confidence in any situation, skill or combination of skills is never easy. Many people spend a whole lifetime playing golf but without being very effective at it, but as a pastime this matters little. Vocal confidence is going to be key in developing your voice. This was the reasoning behind the early part of this chapter, which set the scene or context for where you are as a young teacher. As with any journey, you have to know your starting point to plan and execute the best route.

However, this does not mean that you will be starting from a point of no confidence. Although Will is not a confident singer, he was confident with his voice, or at least he felt he was. What he began to realise over time was that vocal confidence was more than just continuing to use and be happy with his voice as it was. As his teaching within school developed, he realised that there was far more he could do with his voice to communicate effectively.

Confidence is needed to start this journey, if we can see it as that, to understand what we are or are not confident with in relation to our voices. So, what are the basics of how the voice works and what key components will help us on this journey?

We have identified three key areas within which the 'anatomy' of your voice can be explored:

1. The fuel of your voice: air.

2. The buzz of your voice: your voice box.

3. The amplification of your voice: throat, nose, chest, mouth and sinuses.

1. The fuel of your voice

Air not only keeps you alive, it is also the 'life' of your voice! Without the regular flow of air as a starting point there is no voice. Your voice is essentially a wind instrument, very similar to a brass instrument in many ways.

Vocal development is strongly linked to this air flow, including the amount of air, the speed of air and the support of air. Breathing is an obvious place to start. It is something that we do naturally, in fact so naturally that you have done it since the day you were born and have probably taken it for granted! A small part of your brain – the amygdala – deals with this. It is the first and most basic function of your brain, to keep you alive. It also does more complex things like monitor your blood pressure, work to scan your environment for safety and control (what some call the 'fight, flight or freeze' instinct), but it also keeps you breathing day and night.

As it comes naturally, many of us won't spend much time thinking about our breathing. Why would you! You have other things to think about on a daily basis. To the untrained eye, it is also difficult to note and observe what we are doing well or incorrectly in respect to our breathing. Therefore, there is a huge amount of untapped potential in our lungs. A good teacher will help you develop this. So, let's just take a moment to breathe.

Stand for a moment and place your hand on your belly button. Breathe in and out several times. This will hopefully relax you too if you are reading this in some free time or after a long day at work. As you breathe, try to feel what in your body is going in and out. What you are technically trying to do is breathe using your diaphragm more effectively. Imagine a band around your waist that you are trying to stretch while breathing in. Don't force this though, it might not feel natural or come instantly to you. Try to keep your posture relaxed but like your mum or perhaps your grandma told you, 'stand up straight'. The more relaxed and natural you are in terms of a good posture, with the body parts more naturally aligned, the more easily the air will flow in and out of your body. If you want to, try screwing yourself up in a ball on the floor and breathing deeply. It is next to impossible!

PRACTICAL TASK 1

Put aside a few minutes of each day to focus on breathing, posture and staying relaxed. It is a great way to start your day! One of the best and favourite singers we work with, Wayne Ellington, would even recommend linking this to some meditation to develop even more awareness of your own self. This often starts with breathing exercises.

It is important to realise that we are not trying to control or change your breathing. This will more likely result in increased tension and erratic breathing rather than improving it. Try to harness your natural way of breathing and understand it more. Try to relax the muscles that support this. Muscles are essentially designed to contract, then you relax them. If muscles stay in a state of contraction this will lead to pain. So, try to realise what the natural habits are that get in the way of your breathing and what you can do naturally to breathe more deeply.

As you breathe think of trying to fill the bottom of your lungs first, as odd a concept as this may strike you. It will encourage you to think about deeper breathing and the posture linked to this. As you stand try to feel relaxed with your shoulders back, find your natural balance point, try to be aware of the weight of your body pushing you down to the floor, try to keep everything relaxed with the only tension coming in your diaphragm to push your belt out and fill your lungs with air.

PRACTICAL TASK 2

Try repeating Practical Task 1 whilst lying down. This will help you put your shoulders back and align your body. Try counting in your head as you breathe, developing an ability to breathe in over 4 counts and breathe out over 4. Try to develop this over time so that you can evenly do in over 6 and out over 6, moving slowly on to in over 12 and out over 12.

Again, follow the tips from above. Be aware of your body and your breathing. Fill your lungs slowly. Try to not have any tension in the body whilst doing this. Try to enhance your natural breathing and develop it, not force your body to breathe in a way that is unnatural.

As you feel you get a little more proficient at this try to consider the amount of air, not just the speed of air that enters and leaves you body. As you relax and expand your trachea try to feel how much air you can get into your body and out. Not just breathing quickly but breathing deeply.

So, as you breathe in, your diaphragm lowers, your rib cage expands and the lungs fill with air. The opposite happens as you breathe out. As you develop your voice though, the amount of air not just the speed of this will be key. We will return to this several times when we are considering the sound you make and how you can control key elements such as pitch but also dynamics, timbre, pace, rhythm and 'size' of voice.

It is important to acknowledge at this point that there are a lot of misconceptions about how we breathe. Will was taught some years ago about diaphragm control and how it is used to support the air coming out of your body, i.e. that you use your diaphragm to breathe out. This is incorrect, as Jacobson notes, 'the diaphragm has no nerve endings or sensation. Additionally, the diaphragm is primarily a muscle of inspiration and consequently plays very little role in exhalation rendering the idea of "diaphragmatic support" to be without basis in scientific fact' (Jacobson 2015).

Anyone who has their own children or has done any teaching themselves, will have developed some control of their voice dynamics over time. Even at an early stage in life we often have to learn to shout a little louder if we want to be heard. The control of the breath is key in this. The speed of air will control the volume (dynamic) of the voice. The quicker the air is leaving the body and travelling through the voice box (the noise making bit) the louder it will be. But have you ever noticed that when some people shout it seems ineffective; it has no real impact? Yet, we all remember someone from school or work who, when they shout, stops everyone in their tracks. The main reason for this will be volume of air passing through their anatomy, not just the speed. If the speed of the air flow contributes to the volume of your voice, the amount of air flowing through relates to the size of the sound that you can make. To help you to see what we mean in your own mind, we will explain this with a couple of examples.

Think of your voice pipe, windpipe or trachea as a pipe with a diameter. The larger the diameter of the 'pipe' the greater amount of air that can pass down it at one time. So, a large pipe will give out more air than a small pipe even if the air speed through the pipe is the same. If this amount of air was applied to a reed, piece of grass or voice box, it would buzz (we'll go into more detail about this later in the chapter). Both pipes would produce a similar volume but the larger amount of air will produce a bigger sound.

This is perhaps even better demonstrated by an example we came across in a school recently. The assembly hall was full of several hundred students. The Halle Orchestra had been invited to the school to play for a special assembly for the whole of Key Stage 3. The idea was to introduce the pupils to a musical ensemble they may not have heard before or one that they may not have really engaged with. The orchestra played several pieces, led by Sir Mark Elder, who also communicated fabulously with the pupils. The pupils enjoyed the loud music but, as Mark explained to the students, musical ideas can also be played very quietly. He got the whole orchestra to play very quietly by holding some sustained chords. The sound of the orchestra was amazing and you could imagine the quiet sound passing around the hall and through the students. It was the first time that they had experienced a **huge quiet sound**. It had an impact that most of them have never forgotten. It is not the same as just turning the volume up on a computer or television sound bar! This was completely different musically and physically. It is an amazing experience to have so much air coming at you at such a small speed. The perfect example of slow air but with lots of it!

We don't recommend shouting as a key part of any teacher's vocal repertoire, but if you want to shout and use it as an effective tool for a short amount of time (without ruining your voice, as we'll discuss below), think amount and not just speed of air. This will stop people in their tracks much more effectively.

PRACTICAL TASK 3

Try to be conscious of the amount of air coming from your lungs and thorough your voice pipe, not just the speed of it. Try to practise changing this. Done well, the air will not feel like it is coming from your lungs but from the base of your chest or stomach.

Your breathing and air will also be controlled by other external factors. When we are nervous, anxious, under pressure, worried or scared, our breathing will quicken and become more shallow. So, learning to work with and control your breathing will have more than one beneficial factor. When we work with our student teachers to consider and understand these effects we often ask them to artificially raise their breathing rate or 'nervous state', to better consider what is happening physically. This can be done quickly and effectively by taking a short amount of exercise; something to get you out of breath. It can then be useful to work out how they can use their breathing to calm themselves and bring their feelings back under control.

Air is the fuel of your voice. Taking more air in, supporting and controlling it will make huge differences to your teaching voice. You need to begin learning these processes by harnessing your natural breathing and working with it, developing it in line with your body rather than working against what your body wants to do.

Work to gain a better understanding of how you breathe and, if necessary, what might be stopping you taking deep, natural breaths. Watch out for tension. Tension, pain or ache in any muscles are a sign of not being relaxed. The following key bullet points will help you develop your breathing technique further:

Breath control symptoms

Try and avoid doing the following:

- Audible inspiration or 'gasping' on inspiration;

- Running out of air on a sentence;

- Shallow breathing;

- Raising/lowering the shoulders on inspiration/expiration.

Breathing for speech

When speaking, think about when you take a breath. The following signs may indicate that you need to think harder about when to breathe, or how to breathe more deeply using the techniques we have discussed above:

- Does your upper chest area move forward on each breath?

- Do your shoulders rise slightly?

- Do you run out of air whilst talking?

- Does your throat hurt whilst talking loudly?

- Does your voice drop off towards the end of a phrase?

More positively, when breathing:

- Keep your shoulders and upper chest relaxed during speech;

- Focus on coordinating your breath with your speech;

- Speak slowly, pausing often at natural phrase boundaries, to allow the replenishment of breath;

- Avoid squeezing out the last few words without sufficient breath;

- Breathe from your diaphragm rather than using your upper chest as this is a more efficient way of breathing.

Breathing for voice

Efficient breathing for voice production is characterised by the following features:

- Silent oral inspiration of air;

- Quick oral inspiration and slow exhalation of air in a rhythmic pattern;

- Relaxation and expansion of the lower ribs and lower chest area on inspiration of air;

- Little or no movement of the upper chest and shoulders on inspiration of air;

- A focus on exhalation of air rather than on inspiration so that inspiration is automatic and relaxed;

- Release of breath either simultaneously with or just before the onset of voice – not too early or too late;

- Pausing as soon as there are signs that you are about to run out of breath so that inspiration of air will occur automatically for the next phrase;

- Regulation of breath supply to coordinate with the length of phrases – take sufficient air in for the amount you wish to say in each utterance. (Magic of Voice 2013)

2. The buzz of your voice

Your voice box or larynx is at the top of this pipe that we have been mentioning in the previous section. So, the air you are pushing goes through this. It contains two vocal folds (also known as vocal cords) that open during breathing and close during swallowing and voice production. To produce sound, or your voice, these two folds come together to vibrate and make a 'buzz'. Why call it a buzz? Well, it's similar to that which is used to produce the sound in a brass instrument, so this will be a useful example as it is something that we can see as well as hear more easily.

If you play, have played or even had a go at school at playing a brass instrument you will know the basics of how the sound is made. The lips are brought together and air is pushed from your body to make the instrument vibrate or buzz. This often starts with some comical trump sounds but as you get control of your lips it can be more described as a buzz and used less for its potential comic value! Try this, you probably already have. The tightness of the lips, controlled by the muscles in your face will allow you to make the buzz go to a higher or lower pitch, technically increasing or decreasing the amount of vibrations per second. This is very similar to what happens in your voice box as the air passes through the vocal folds. These can vibrate very quickly, controlled by the muscles, to produce between 100 and 1000 vibrations per second. This is the start of your voice or the sound you make.

The pitch of the voice will be controlled by the tightness of the vocal cords, which are controlled by muscles in the larynx. So, like an experienced brass player, the buzz is the start of the sound; the amount of and speed of air through the buzz will also contribute to the dynamic and the size of sound. As we practise this over time, we can develop better control of these muscles to gain better pitch, timbre, dynamic and overall vocal control.

The muscular memory that you develop over time is what will help you move from making gurgling sounds as a baby, to producing phonemes, to moving these phonemes into sounds and these sounds into words. It is not an easy process but is actually a very natural one. Most babies don't need formal instruction to learn how to speak!

As with learning to play a musical instrument, you will need to begin to understand more thoroughly what your voice box is and how you can use it to help develop a larger range of vocal sounds and interactions. Like any skill, the more proficient you become with it the more able you will be at calling upon it at a particular moment and for a particular purpose. Like a more proficient musician, you will learn to develop a greater range of pitch, dynamic, control, timbre. You will be able to move more quickly throughout your range or skills and be able to use these specifically to make the instrument, your voice, do exactly what you want it to do at any given moment.

PRACTICAL TASK 4

Repeat the breathing exercises from earlier in the chapter. Engage the voice box. 'Hum' to yourself supporting a single pitch. Breathe in over four and then hum out over four. Try to control this pitch and size of sound.

Try to spend a few minutes a day doing this. Don't concern yourself if you find this difficult. Focus on the air, the speed of air, and the amount of air within your breathing. Pushing the air from your body in a steady, even stream is not easy. But it is something you can develop. Try to view this as a whole body experience. Making a sound *is* a whole body experience.

Try to combine these sounds with the natural breathing of the early exercise. Try to sense and work with, not against, your body. Even if you notice tension or perceived problems, work slowly at eradicating or changing these, making small subtle changes. Try things that you feel may not work. Try sitting or standing differently, moving your head around in small amounts.

One of the key things linked to breathing and air is nerves or being nervous. As we mentioned earlier, your amygdala controls your breathing alongside the 'staying alive' functions of your neural activity. Being concerned in your mind about your voice will bring on the same anxieties we mentioned about being nervous, anxious or stressed. Your voice can be affected. As you became increasingly nervous of your voice, you try to hide it and you worry about being caught. Your brain will prepare for 'flight' mode. It will have increased your heart rate for increased oxygen to your muscles, your eyes will widen to spot danger, your breathing speed will increase in preparation. I'm sure most of us have been told in various situations to relax, breathe deeply and try to control our nerves. Understanding how your breath can be supported and delivered in a smooth manner will not only support your vocal confidence, but also your ability to feel more confident in stressful situations – like teaching!

So, get practising breathing! This will not only support your voice, voice production and confidence but could also have very positive effects on other aspects of your daily life too. Try to become more metacognitive of these skills, thereby learning to control them and use them more effectively.

REFLECTIVE TASK

Research some YouTube videos for other vocal exercises that you feel comfortable with. Remember, this is not about becoming a great singer or focussing on making quick improvements. It is really key here to not focus on trying to develop your voice, confidence or understanding at speed. Have fun trying to understand the basic concepts of air speed, amount of air and how your buzz adds sound to this. Focussing on any problems or things you feel you can't do will only have the opposite effect of what this chapter and book are about.

There is no quick fix for this type of work. Even the first step of breathing more from your diaphragm can take time to understand, conceptualise and use. Build exercises into your everyday routine. Make it enjoyable! This will mean you will be relaxed and confident that progress is being made, however slow and steady that progress is.

3. The amplification of your voice

Our brass playing friends use their lips to produce the buzz of sound. Air passing between the lips controlled by the tension of the facial muscles controls the speed of vibration, quality of buzz and size of sound. This buzz is aimed into a mouthpiece; this directs the air down a smaller tube into the brass instrument. So what does the instrument do?

Well, the bore of the instrument is very cleverly designed to affect the sound it makes. Some brass instruments have cylindrical bores, which essentially means that the tubing stays at a constant size until the end when the bell will open to spread the sound. The trombone is a good example of this as the slide that lengthens it will only work if the bore of it stays constant. The trumpet is also very similar but with valves. The instruments are characterised as having a strident or more forceful sound.

Many of the other brass instruments, for instance in a brass band, have conical bores, this means that the bore opens virtually constantly, increasing in size from mouthpiece to bell, although this is not absolutely true as the air goes through the valves. These instruments are more rounded in sound, less strident and more mellow. They also have a varied bell size, which helps to amplify the sound.

So, you might at this point be asking why you are getting such an in-depth brass lesson? Well, as before, it is a good way of visualising how your voice works with things that you can actually see, e.g. the component parts of a musical instrument. As we have discussed already, one of the main issues with voice production and control is to understand what is making the sound and how it is affected.

The buzz has been created in your body by your voice box, by air passing through the vocal cords. By themselves they produce a sound similar to that of the buzz of the lips. You can easily hear how the mouthpiece, instrument bore, size, bell and shape change this in a brass instrument. Your body is the same. We all have a unique voice, although some are excellent at copying or mimicking others. Voice coaches even specialise in copying famous voices, or accents or even regional dialects. So, how? How much do we need to know to develop our understanding of our own voice and thus use it more effectively?

Well, the throat, nose, chest, mouth, tongue and sinuses will all have a major effect on the sound you produce and how your voice is heard. Just trying saying an 'eee' sound and then an 'oooo' sound. Can you feel or spot where those sounds are made? Where they resonate? Where they simply cause vibrations?

To make the 'eee' sound raise your tongue to the upper part of your mouth. It resonates in the sinuses and nose. To make the 'ooo' sound, as you drop your tongue the sound more readily resonates in the chest. Try also varying the pitch of these 'eee' and 'ooo' sounds to try and feel where they happen and where you can position them.

Your head position is also key in this. As Jacobson explains:

> The larynx hangs from the hyoid bone which is slung from the mastoid processes on the skull. If the head is pulled down into the spine, the neck and throat muscles will be tense and the torso will become rigid. Excess tension kills vibrations and will produce a sound that is tight and strained.
>
> (Jacobson 2015)

Whilst doing the exercises from earlier, try to notice more where the sound is produced, where it sits and where it feels like it resonates. It should be obvious that this will not be the same for all of us. Like the varying brass instruments, we are all shaped differently so this will change our sound. But because our body is flesh, muscle, tissue, etc., unlike a brass instrument, we have the ability to change this far more. Over time we can control more and more how the sound is produced, where it resonates and thus how it sounds. You can only best do this by experimenting, but try noticing how others do it, too.

To that end, listen attentively to people you work with or spend time with at home. Where do you feel they produce their voice? Would you characterise it as a nasal voice, or chest voice, does it sound like it comes from a wide or narrow pipe, does it carry around the house as a big voice, or is it just loud?

The idea is just to become increasingly aware of how this resonating chamber of physical parts affects the final sound we can make. More importantly though, how changing the shape, use and position of these can affect our own sound.

By active experimentation with these three key components – air, buzz and amplification – you will begin to discover a whole new range of vocal sound and delivery. From our experience, the biggest problem most people have is with air. It is the easiest thing to forget and the most vital to work on. The combination of throat, nose, chest, mouth and sinuses to amplify your voice is key to the most important step of being happy with the sound your voice makes.

It wasn't long ago that we were listening to Sam Smith, the popular singer, and Rod Stewart, the ever young British rock singer. Both of these have quite distinctive voices, very easy in many ways to pick out from the crowd.

Sam Smith could be characterised as having a very nasal sound, producing his sounds 'high' in his head again using his nasal area and upper face. If you watch him his upper face seems to work hard for the sound with less visible movement in the neck or chest.

Rod Stewart has a distinctive raspy voice. The sound feels quite tight and forced in some ways. We often feel ourselves wanting to clear our throats when listening to him! If you watch him his voice is still very nasal in some ways but there is more movement in his neck and the sound is stronger, with more air.

We chose these two examples for two reasons. First, we don't particularly like either of their singing voices (although Will's dad would kill me for having any sort of *dig* at the Rod Stewart classic 'I am sailing'). Second, they both have very distinctive voices. So it gives us something to analyse but more importantly it allows us to realise that whether we like their voices or not is irrelevant. Whether you or anyone else does is largely irrelevant too! The only key point is **they like their voices**. We could ask many vocal coaches to analyse both voices and tell you their strengths and faults, but they are both confident singers, performers and use their voices amazingly. But for us, one key point resonates more than any other: they like the sound they make. **They. Like. The sound. They make.**

That's what you've got to get to start having! More confidence in your own voice!

PRACTICAL TASK 5

Use a portable recording device such as a mobile phone to record your own voice. Try and do this in several different situations. Listen back to yourself. First, be happy with the sound you make, It's what makes you uniquely you. But then try to start to analyse how you make your sound. Go through the key components of air, buzz and amplification. How does it change in varying situations? Look at what moves and how much. Then try different ideas.

The whole point of this important chapter is to try to help you gain more understanding of how the key parts of your voice work together to make the sound that is you. As we have seen, it starts with how you breathe – a good air speed and volume. The muscular control affects the buzz. Then how the amplification of that sound is affected by all the nuances of throat, nose, mouth, tongue, lips and the chambers where the sound resonates.

Developing your voice is all about your vocal confidence. It is a natural process but it takes mindful practice. You need to continue to develop your expression, communication and understanding in a natural manner that works in conjunction with your body. It is important that you allow yourself to make mistakes, whatever you perceive these mistakes to be. Like young children learning and developing their language, mistakes are irrelevant. It's all about your development; focus on the journey not the destination. As we have realised with our own children, if we want them to develop confidence and understanding in their own abilities, they have to be allowed to make mistakes.

To conclude this chapter and hopefully engage you to want to go on further with the development of your voice, let's consider some key points from Victor Wooten:

■ Embrace mistakes. They aren't mistakes! It's just about gaining more understanding of how you make your sound.

■ A language works best when we have something interesting to say – this is related not to just what we say but how we say it. Developing confidence and a greater vocal range will allow you to 'be more interesting'.

■ Too many rules at the onset will hinder not help – start from where you are. Develop your breathing, sound and voice naturally. Don't set expectations, even in your mind, of what you should or shouldn't be able to do or sound like. Just enjoy developing.

(Wooten 2012)

Everyone has a voice to develop, and although some will find this easier to develop than others, everyone, and every teacher, can improve their vocal delivery with positive results.

References

Jacobson, Peter (2015) '9 Things Singers Need to Know about their Bodies'. http://www. totalvocalfreedom.com/9-things-singers-need-know-bodies/ [last accessed 1/3/2017].

Magic of Voice (2013) 'Your voice can change the world'. https://magicofvoice.wordpress. com/2013/08/29/posture/ [last accessed 19/5/17]

Oaklander, M. (2016) 'Science explains why you love Morgan Freeman's voice'. http://time.com/ 4233926/morgan-freeman-voice-waze-science/ [last accessed 21/3/17].

Wooten, Victor (2006) *The Music Lesson.* London: Penguin Books Ltd.
Wooten, Victor (2012) 'Music as a Language'. http://ed.ted.com/lessons/victor-wooten-music-as-a-language [last accessed 3/3/2017].

Chapter 3

Your voice and your pedagogy

Richard Burton was one of 13 children brought up in a Welsh speaking home in Pontrhydyfen. He would go on to have one of the most characteristic voices in British film history, being nominated seven times for an Oscar.

His voice is deep in pitch and well supported with air. In simple language, he is putting through as much air as though he was shouting loudly, but doing this slowly so it is a big sound, not a loud sound. At a young age in such a large family he would have been surrounded by lots of 'expert' speakers. There would have been little time for individual support so you can bet that to be heard in such a large group you had to quickly develop your own voice and willingness to speak up.

The Welsh are well known as singers, demonstrated through their male voice choirs, mining songs and associated national pride at events such as rugby matches at the Millennium Stadium. It is likely then that singing was a key part of Richard's younger years. He would have been encouraged to develop vocal support and confidence without even knowing it.

Burton was quoted to have said about his family that, 'our voices were born with coal dust and rain' (Quirke 2017). During the 1920s and 1930s, Welsh families would have been regular church goers. Once a week, at least, the young Richard would sit listening to excellent vocal communicators from the pulpit. He would also have participated in congregational singing of hymns with their stirring melodies and harmonies.

When he got to secondary school age, Richard moved to Port Talbot to live with his sister. He met Philip Burton, a frustrated actor and BBC producer who would become his producer, mentor and guardian. He began to work with Richard and to strengthen his voice would take him walking and have him shouting in the hills. Over time, Burton helped Richard increase the amount and speed of air that he would use for his voice. He also helped Burton lose part of his Welsh accent and develop a more relaxed, inviting voice whilst still maintaining elements of his dialect.

All of these factors combined together to develop his distinct style of voice. The low pitch and large amount of air is combined with a subtle use of tempo. Timbre and dynamics are used to empathise text and for dramatic effect. You can sense a confidence, sincerity and integrity to his voice that led one commentator to say that 'his voice – low, measured, weary, full of the sound of cigarettes, women and condensation in martini glasses – is his gift to us' (ibid.).

Suggested listening: Richard Burton reads Churchill's 'Blood, toil, tears & sweat' https://wn.com/richard_burton_reads_churchill's_blood,_toil,_tears_sweat _speech

Here's a bold statement: if you are the most interesting thing in the room, your students will listen to every word you say! Your voice is your most important form of communication. From it, your style of teaching, your pedagogy, can be developed in productive ways that enable you to teach skilfully and through which your students' learning will flourish. This chapter will help you develop ideas about how your voice links closely to your wider teaching skills, and how development of both is inextricably linked.

In the previous chapter we presented the idea that the voice is made up of three main components – the air, the buzz and the amplification. Obviously, these link together as a whole 'voice' that is closely linked to your identity as a human being and a teacher (something we explored in detail in Chapter 1). Ultimately, and in a physiological sense, it is the muscles and shapes of the head, neck and upper body that work together to make your voice sound the way it does. The reason we focussed on the three main elements in the way that we did was to give you a 'handle' on your voice and its component parts, and through this to help you develop a richer and more compelling vocal sound for use within the classroom.

In our work helping young teachers, one of the greatest concerns expressed to us is, 'What shall I do if they all ignore me?' This is a very common anxiety and in our experience not solely restricted to teachers in the United Kingdom or even to the teaching profession. If you have ever been asked to talk in public perhaps you will have felt a similar sense of anxiety. Many of the worries felt by people who have been asked to speak at a social occasion, present ideas at a meeting or make a formal speech are associated with 'being interesting'.

We often joke with trainee teachers that this is the easiest thing to do. If you are the most interesting thing in the room, students will listen to every word you have to say. But how do you 'be interesting'. Thinking beyond just 'being interesting', teaching is more than just getting students to listen to you isn't it? It is about communicating, enabling the cognitive processes in other people's brains; it's about engaging them in the learning experience so that they learn things in diverse ways, and not just so that you can teach.

REFLECTIVE TASK

Who do you find interesting to listen to? Make a list of the key attributes, skills or abilities that they have. Do these things change depending on when or where they are speaking?

In terms of 'being interesting', there are reasons why your voice is important. Whilst what you say is important, how you say it is fundamental to the way in which ideas are received by others. We will take some time in this chapter to consider what these key factors are. We will then consider how this more deeply connects to your pedagogy and how this might affect it in a positive or negative way.

Teaching is a complex art. In fact, it seems to get ever more complex the more we know about it! Ian Gilbert in Curran (2008) discussed the importance of simplicity and gives an example of how Bill Clinton, when running for US president, would leave himself written reminders that no matter how complex a problem seemed it could always be brought down to a simpler level. He goes onto link this to the work he does with teachers:

> I urge them to do something similar [to President Clinton] for their staffroom door, only this time the sticker should read, 'It's the brain, stupid!' Everything that goes on in a classroom, for better or worse, is a result of activity between the ears. And if you understand that, then no matter how complicated and difficult things get, you have a chance to do something about it.
>
> (Gilbert in Curran 2008, p. 82)

To take Gilbert's idea a little further, we need to unpick it and relate it to our topic of the voice and pedagogy. We need to consider the idea of learning, what learning actually is, what chemical and electrical connections go on with every thought, feeling, movement and idea that happens in every moment of your life. What is happening in your brain as you go about your daily life? Whilst you are reading this book? Observing your students arriving for your lesson? In Chapter 4, Curran writes about 'making those chemicals dance to a learning beat' and distils this into four main ideas:

UNDERSTAND the human in front of you. Then you will improve their SELF-ESTEEM. If you do this you will improve their SELF-CONFIDENCE. And if you do that, they will feel EMOTIONALLY ENGAGED by what you are doing.

(ibid.)

Perhaps this is what Curran means by being interesting. The point to start us off here though is that the brain is constantly monitoring not just what you say, but how you say it. Before we are ready for learning, according to Curran, our brain is doing two things. Firstly, its main focus is on keeping us alive, everything from the basics of breathing, as we mentioned in the previous chapter, to surveying the surrounding areas for threats (big tigers!) that might kill us (usually not too much of a problem in our local area). When it is done with that, it can move on. Secondly, the brain is wired to keep the human race alive, to find a mate and make sure that the human survives a little longer. After it's done with these it then has some space for learning, for what is happening in your classroom.

So, this is why it is going to be key to be interesting, especially for those working in secondary schools when faced with 30 social-media friendly and energy-drink fuelled teenagers. Your voice is your first chance to do this. Your voice sets the mood in your classroom and for your interactions with others within it. Your voice allows you to set into motion Andrew Curran's main points for learning to happen. It is crucial to consider that lessons that start with several minutes of 'barked' instructions not only affect you as a teacher, the students as human beings, but also affect how ready their brains will be to learn.

So, no wonder people who are starting on this journey are worried. We seem in many ways to be set up to fail. If the only model we have seen, and the only technique that we have at the beginning of lesson, is to shout at children to get their attention, we have failed already. The varying of the voice is crucial to effective teaching and can be used, like a great artist, to produce a pallet of colours and shades of light and dark.

At the beginning of a teacher's training and development, there is a clear focus on the skills of teaching. This is logical and sensible in many ways and most young teachers could make a list of skills that they have been introduced to and practised. These would include things like:

■ The curriculum for your subject(s);

■ Learning to set appropriate learning objectives;

■ Preparing and organising resources for lessons;

■ Planning interesting teaching activities within lessons that help students meet those learning objectives;

■ Evaluating lessons to make improvements to your own teaching and, hopefully, the students' learning too;

■ Assessing students' work in a variety of ways;

■ Making observations of teaching to learn from others.

However, we must be careful not to reduce teaching to just a list of skills that can be simply practised. There is much in this but teaching is itself an art. By this, we mean it is the teacher, in the act of teaching, that will turn the bullet points above into an art, into a lesson that engages others and enables, over time, learning to occur.

Through our work with trainee teachers over the past 15 years it has become clear to us how the development of your voice in conjunction with your pedagogy is crucial to your progress as a young teacher.

Making a start

As we begin teaching, our focus is often on issues associated with behaviour and classroom management, controlling the classroom and its resources, and delivering the list of activities or tasks set out in the lesson plan. This is completed with varying degrees of success. In our work with young teachers, we often break this into four key points for our students to focus on:

1. Get them in.

2. Get on with it.

3. Get on with them.

4. Get them out.

Consider three things you might do at a lesson start.

1. Give instructions to the whole class to get them in, sorted and settled.

2. Ask questions to individuals to engage them, encourage them to settle and to begin some personal interaction.

3. Model to the whole class the main task of the lesson, including asking whole class questions.

For a moment, see yourself, or a colleague, in these situations. What 'voice' is needed for each one? Is it the same? Does it have the same timbre, intonation, pitch, size, dynamic? How could varying these help to support or negate communication in these situations?

Amazingly, if you make these observations (and, over time, we have made hundreds of such observations of teachers), you will see a marked difference in how more experienced teachers communicate. More importantly, you will notice how lack of thinking and planning for how the voice is used is common amongst younger teachers. Let's take each of the three points in turn.

1. Give instructions to the whole class to get them in, sorted and settled

This needs a big voice, plenty of air coming from the lungs, supported by the diaphragm to fill the room, but more importantly to make sure everyone can hear what you are saying. Fast air, volume, should be avoided apart from in very small moments, for effect. If the air is moving too fast, it will give a sense of shouting, even losing control, and the students often sense this. *It may be the brain preparing for a kill!* Pace should be slow, or feel slow in your head. Keep the pitch reasonably low, this will also help your voice to fill the room. Use the pitch and rhythm of voice to model the key thought that you want the pupils to hurry, settle and get sorted. Make sure your voice begins to modulate and settle as they physically do the same.

2. Ask questions to individuals to engage them, encourage them to settle and to begin some personal interaction

This may need to be done as interludes, interjections and asides to the first point. The voice will instantly need to be smaller, i.e. have a smaller amount of air flowing from the lungs supported by the diaphragm. The intonation should vary more and encourage the individual to listen. The pitch and timbre of your voice should encourage answers but with the pace that this is done quickly so that the individuals join with the mass to settle quickly.

3. Model to the whole class the main task of the lesson, including asking whole class questions

This is where the voice has to change. We are moving beyond instructions to engagement, to learning. We need the students to wake the mass of grey between their ears and begin to make connections. The brain needs to be engaged beyond its two primary functions and engagement with your voice will be key to this. What you are communicating must not only be important but sound important. Variety is key to engagement here. It must vary to include different thinkers, listeners and students in the room. It must fill the space but also 'draw pupils in'. It is where the biggest consideration of air speed, air amount, pitch, rhythm, timbre, dynamic must be given.

So, to make a start on how you would like to develop your own voice for teaching it is important to consider the three scenarios introduced above. You may also have others situations that you have come across that create anxiety or specific challenges. For these, consider what the voice needs to be like; try to hear this in your mind. Can you analyse what is happening? The more experienced teachers here will probably find they have some ideas but those beginning on the journey might find it more challenging.

PRACTICAL TASK

Try and observe a range of teachers in varying situations using their voice. You can even do this partly by watching videos of people teaching online, although you don't always get the whole impact here. Try to consider before you observe which elements of voice you are trying to notice and how this will relate to your practice.

Try to separate the teacher's vocal delivery from the other aspects of the work. Observe and consider:

1. How is *air* used? How often does the person breathe and how. How are breaths (their breathing) built into what they are doing? How much air is leaving the body through the voice box? Is the voice big (remember here that should not be confused with being loud, that's about air speed)? How do they support the voice? Does the air flow keep going to support the voice? How can you tell? How is air speed used to vary the dynamic of the voice? When are louder dynamics used to good or lesser effect? When are quieter dynamics used to good or lesser effect?

2. How is the *pitch* of voice used? This is especially crucial in teachers starting their careers. We have noticed so many times that with the stress of the first teaching experiences, the vocal pitch is likely to rise to a quite annoying level. Adding to the problem, it often stays there for several minutes with little variation. What does this do to the students trying to listen? What would happen if you were listening to a song that stayed in a similar pitch for a sustained amount of time? It is very important to notice this as the variations of pitch are least likely, in our experience, to feel normal. During everyday life our voice has a natural pitch; it isn't natural at all but years and years of practice have found this comfortable pitch for us, which is different for all of us. Most likely as you begin to teach though this pitch will rise to compensate for volume or size of voice. Pitch is much easier to vary than working to take in more and more air and then support this on its way out.

3. Focus on *pitch variation*. Are there any natural variations in the teacher's voice? Is there any useful correlation between vocal pitch and activity or communication?

4. Where does the voice *resonate*? Does the person you are observing seem to have a nasal voice or chest voice? Does the voice seem too light and high in the head or deep in the chest? Is there any notable movement in the neck

or head area that gives any indication? Is there variation in this? Do any male teachers vary between a type of falsetto and their adult male voice?

5. How are the teeth and mouth used to shape words, give diction and clarity?

Make some notes on observations you make and, if possible, try to discuss them at a later point with the teachers you have observed. It may be interesting for them to consider but also interesting for you as your reflect on the voice that you are forming for your own teaching.

Planning

Most successful lessons begin with a well constructed lesson plan. Although our students often moan about their planning, it is our strong contention that planning a good lesson is an essential first step to teaching a good lesson. As we discussed above, what is normally meant by a lesson plan is the core components of a lesson including learning objectives, teaching activities, assessment or differentiation strategies, resources, etc. We would like to extend this process, by asking you to consider what you will want to say during a lesson and how your are proposing to say it.

However, therein lies a problem. As any speech writer will tell you, there are clear differences between written and spoken language. These are equally important for the lesson planning process. It is usually the case, is it not, that when you are thinking about planning a lesson you are sitting on your own, pen in hand or in front of the computer, and you begin the process by writing? This act, in itself, has important consequences for your ideas and how they are communicated. Drawing on the work of David Shirley, Principal Lecturer in Drama at Manchester Metropolitan University, here are some of the key differences for you to consider.

1. The rules of grammar tend to be applied much more rigorously when it comes to *written* language. The need for carefully structured and well thought out sentences forms an important part of this mode of communication. The same is not true, however, of *spoken* language, which as a result of its 'liveness' and 'spontaneity' tends to be more relaxed and less formal.

2. The words and phrases that we use in our classroom talk are the tools with which we communicate ideas, shape new impressions and generate meaning. When writing ideas down in a lesson plan, there is a strong tendency to deploy words that are generally more technical than those used in everyday conversation. When writing, the ideas can be communicated with clarity and precision. As soon as the words are embodied by ourselves as a teacher and delivered in *spoken* language, all other aspects of communication come into play – such as your personality,

intonation, rhythm, body language, eye contact, etc. All of these factors will help to impart the general impressions that your students will have of you. If your language in the lesson is overly formal, technical or precise (i.e. as it was formulated within your lesson plan), the danger is that your students may view you as too stiff and formal rather than being relaxed and at ease with your teaching role.

3. A common feature of written language is that sentences can be long and complex. This is, perhaps, one of the key strengths of planning a lesson on paper (or the screen) in advance of delivering it to your students. It allows you time to reflect on the ideas and re-read phrases/sentences that may be complex and help you consider how to present these within the lesson. However, the converse is true. *Spoken* language makes it almost impossible to recapture lost thoughts so it is important when structuring your speech in a lesson that arguments, thoughts and ideas are presented in shorter, well punctuated and carefully balanced sentences.

4. Whereas in *written* language repetition is often perceived as a weakness, the reverse is true of spoken language. The repeated emphasis of key ideas within a lesson can help both to drive home an important message and provide a bridge between the key thoughts relating to one's own ideas and those of others (i.e. your students). Indeed, the skilled use of repetition as a rhetorical device is often a hallmark of what might be termed 'great' public speaking (by the way, did you listen to Richard Burton's rendition of that great Winston Churchill speech linked at the end of this chapter's iconic voice portrait?).

So, to summarise, there is a need for simplicity when it comes to effective spoken language. This is not because your audience, your students, may or may not be capable of digesting and understanding in-depth ideas or complex-thought structures. But it is about you being able to understand the distinctions between the planning processes that you have to undertake as a teacher and that are normally done in writing, against the immediacy and conventions of the spoken word that have to be delivered through skilful oration within the lesson itself. As Shirley goes onto say:

> Understanding that the energy and dynamism of live spoken language is often markedly different to that of written text will help promote decisions that are likely to have the best possible impact on the spectator/listener and thereby serve to ensure that the desired objective is achieved.
>
> (Shirley 2017, p. 2)

Speaking as performance

If teaching is an art (and we would argue that it is), it is a *performance* art. The key roles that a teacher plays in the classroom could be related, metaphorically at least, to the role that an actor has to play.

The theatre is a fantastic place that allows actors and audiences to dream together, be taken to new places, to enjoy and be challenged by new experiences. One of the aspirations of any theatre production is that the audience will leave the theatre changed in some way as a result of experiencing that production. This has many similarities to the processes of teaching and learning in the classroom. As teachers, we would all hope that our students do not leave our classrooms in the same state that they entered them! Learning should have occurred and this, over time, will result in cognitive and physical development.

With the exception of the most improvisatory forms of theatre (of which more below), most actors work with a script. In the majority of cases this script is fixed. It contains the words and other directions needed to perform the play according to the desire of the author. In many theatre traditions, e.g. Shakespearian traditions, it would not be considered appropriate to change the words of the play although, of course, many other aspects – such as the context within which the play is set, the staging of the play, the lighting and sound design – could all be developed in ways far from those imagined by the original playwright. However, it is worth pausing and considering whether or not the script, that the actors have to remember and deliver using all their skills, is really 'the play'? As we have already hinted, the words of the script are framed by all kinds of other devices and structures. These would include the larger aspects of artistic direction such as a broader context for the play, the set and sound design, but it would also include elements that are intrinsic to the skills, techniques and work of an individual actor within this framework: the sound of their voice, the pace of their delivery, the emotional input that they impose onto the language, the way that they interact with other actors, and much more besides. Beyond all of these considerations are the audience, who constitute another layer of interaction with which the actor needs to communicate. How they respond to the events that unfold before them has an intrinsic effect on what any individual actor may do. They may 'play to the house' during one performance in a way that they would not do on another occasion. More broadly, certain elements, e.g. set design, are likely to be fixed and unchangeable despite what an audience might think about them.

To what extent is this like the process of planning for teaching? At a basic level, the lesson plan itself could be compared with the script. It contains the key sequences and instructions needed to deliver a lesson. The teacher plays the role of the actor and the classroom becomes the set, the context for the performance that plays a fundamental role in bringing it to life (or not). Finally, of course, the pupils are the audience, invited into this space for a particular performance and engaged and changed, we hope, as a result.

But the metaphor begins to fall apart because it places the teacher in the dual role of author and actor. Initially, the lesson plan has to be imagined and created. It is written by the teacher (author) with a specific group of students in mind, for a specific place (their classroom) at a particular time (Monday morning, period two). As we have seen, all of these aspects (pupils, place and time) need to be considered carefully and the plan needs to reflect that level of specific thinking. It will present a set of ideas through a narrative that has structure (some kind of scene setting leading to the main events of the play), key ideas (characters or topics) and some kind of resolution within a set time period. But, secondly, the teacher is also the actor charged with bringing the script to life within a specific performance event (the lesson). Here, like the actor, they have to bring all their human qualities and attributes to bear in order for the performance to be engaging and convincing.

In Chapter 7 we will consider two other metaphors for the performance of teaching and the ways in which these might impact on our vocal delivery in the classroom. For now, we will consider a few further practical points.

Some further points on vocal delivery

1. Eye contact

One of the most common ways of engaging and sustaining the attention of your students will be by making frequent eye contact with them. If, when speaking to your class, you seldom lift your eyes from your notes, or from your computer screen or the PowerPoint presentation that you have lovingly prepared at 3 a.m. the previous morning, then it is less likely that your students will engage with what you are saying. At one level, the frequent use of eye contact with every student in your class acts as a form of surveillance in that it provides you with clear evidence of how much you are engaged with your students. Clearly, if you are watching your students carefully they might be less inclined to disengage anyway!

At another level, the regular use of eye contact will enable you to measure the impact of your vocal delivery at that point in the lesson, enabling you to make adjustments to what you are saying and how you are saying it. Equally important, frequent use of eye contact with each student individually enhances the credibility of what is being said. If your student is able to see your eyes and meet your gaze, they will feel personally addressed by you as their teacher and will be much more likely to be persuaded or influenced by what you are saying. Clearly, this is going to be vitally important if they are going to learn things from you or with you.

2. Pausing

Pauses and small breaks in vocal delivery provide an invaluable form of punctuation when it comes to communicating ideas and generating new thoughts in your students' minds. Intentional silences that are longer than those used in normal conversation provide a space within which your students can digest new information for themselves, mark important changes in content or recognise a shift in emphasis. Without intentional pauses or breaks of this type, it is hard for students to follow the sequence of new ideas and make sense of these for themselves.

From your point of view as a teacher, the use of pauses or breaks in communication can help you too. You can use them to gather new thoughts, change direction and control your physical presence and your breath. On occasions, you'll be able to measure the extent to which a new idea has been received by students and, where necessary, make decisions in the moment to include additional examples or metaphors to help strengthen their understanding. The use of pauses and breaks in this way can make your vocal delivery more engaging, dynamic and varied.

Incidentally, we note that the changes to electronic forms of presentation have often denied the helpful opportunities that teachers in previous ages would have had through taking the time to write things down on a blackboard or whiteboard. The instantaneous projection of slides electronically does not allow the teacher that important thinking space that can provide this reflective pause. As with any digital tool, there are positive affordances and some less helpful dimensions to their use in a classroom. This provides yet another important and compelling reason to find natural pauses and breaks in your vocal delivery.

3. Intonation and stress

The ability to shift intonation and vary the pattern of stresses in your vocal delivery is at the heart of effective communication. The manner in which an idea is communicated to students is often every bit as important as the idea itself. Passion, enthusiasm, optimism and conviction are all conveyed by the tone that you adopt as a teacher. If, whether intentionally or otherwise, you sound bored then it is hardly reasonable to expect your students to feel differently. It is vitally important to remember that there is a performance dimension to teaching. It is not just an *art*, as we've discussed elsewhere in this chapter, it is also a *performance art*! One of the key arguments of this book is that you can take the voice that you have from your early years, and develop this into a dynamic and engaging teaching voice. Recognising that classroom talk is performative in its nature and thereby larger than everyday conversation, and noting that with continued practice things can improve, you will be able to produce a classroom vocal delivery that has real and lasting benefits for yourself and your vocal health (see Chapter 8) and your students too.

PRACTICAL TASK

Think about a lesson that you are going to teach in the next few weeks where you are going to have to introduce a new concept or idea to your students. Draft an explanation of the concept that you could use within the lesson. Try and ensure that the total explanation is no longer than two to three minutes in total. It is important to make sure that you have completed a full written draft of the explanation in order to do the next parts of the task.

Part 1: Pauses

Work through the explanation and identify possible places at which to pause. Mark the text with slashes using a single slash (/) for a short pause and a double slash (//) for a longer one.

Read through the explanation again testing whether the pauses you have planned are effective or not. It is important to read the explanation aloud (i.e. not in your head). Consider the impact of changing or moving the places where the pauses are identified.

Part 2: Stresses

Read the explanation through a couple of times and identify the key phrases or words that need to be stressed. Identify at least one word in each sentence and underline the chosen word in pencil.

Read the explanation again aloud. Measure the impact of your chosen stresses. If possible, record yourself reading the explanation on a mobile phone or other recording device. Listen back and consider whether your explanation has been enhanced through the stresses you have added.

Part 3: For stress and implication

Take a break from your explanation for this exercise that asks you to place a stress on a different word in a sentence in order to convey a variety of reasons.

Different stresses	Implied meanings
I didn't say you could play my ukulele.	Somebody else may have said it.
I didn't say you could play my ukulele.	I deny it.
I didn't say you could play my ukulele.	I may have thought it.
I didn't say you could play my ukulele.	I gave permission to someone else.
I didn't say you could play my ukulele.	An equivocation.
I didn't say you could play my ukulele.	You could do something else with it.
I didn't say you could play my ukulele.	You could play someone else's.
I didn't say you could play my ukulele.	You could play my ukulele.

Part 4: Intonation

Work your way through the explanation and identify where possible changes of intonation might occur. A good way of doing this is to try and pick out key words or phrases that capture the key impressions within the explanation that you are trying to convey. Examples here may include you wanting to 'motivate', 'encourage' or 'enthuse' your students. Write your chosen words in the margin of your explanation as a reminder of the need to change your intonation.

Again, rehearse and if possible record your explanation. Can you feel a difference in your tone/demeanour as the changes occur?

Read the speech aloud again, but on this occasion exaggerate and heighten the shifts in intonation. How comfortable does this feel and what is the effect on the overall delivery?

Exercise: Eye contact

Using all of the above techniques (pause, stress, intonation), go through the explanation again to identify key points where you will make eye contact with your students. Try and look directly at a number of students during every sentence. Imagine yourself in the classroom, deliver the explanation and count the number of times you are able to make direct eye contact with your [imaginary] students.

Planning, pedagogy and vocal delivery

Jo Salter was the first female jet pilot in Britain. Her account of learning to fly is fascinating reading and illustrates the variety of teaching and learning methods required to become a top pilot. Of particular interest was her account of how you can learn to fly without actually being airborne:

> I used to walk around, rehearsing the checks, the switch positions, the radio calls – running circuits in my bedroom, plotting air defence tactics across a field, circling dogfights on bikes, even flying formation in my sleep. Rehearsal builds muscles in the brain and the brain remembers this much more effectively when flying and operating an aircraft. It is the beginning of an automated sequence where pilots react without thinking – essential for rapid decision-making at life-threatening moments.
>
> (Salter 2005, p. 30)

When Salter began to train as a teacher, she began to relate this process of learning to the challenges associated with teaching:

As a teacher I employ the same lessons that I learnt as a student; I rehearse and visualise – how I am going to stand and how I am going to use my body language in order to convey my message. The spoken word is only part of how we teach. We have all experienced the flat teacher, the one who seems to no longer be there, whose energy has disappeared and whose presence is blurred. These are not the lessons you remember.

(ibid.)

Practice is essential in turning your carefully prepared lesson planning into an exciting and stimulating vocal delivery within the classroom. But practice need not only be done in front of children. You can practise being a teacher all on your own! Salter's pre-rehearsal strategies and visualisation exercises find common ground in the work of actors, musicians, artists and many sports too. There are numerous ways that you can turn your lesson plan into a living enactment of your lesson and pre-lesson rehearsals are a vital part of turning a lesson plan into a reality. So, why not try:

- Reading through, acting out or practising certain key parts of a lesson plan in privacy.

- Structuring explanatory dialogue or key questions and, if necessary, mentally scripting parts of the lesson plan ensuring that there is clarity and purpose in your words. These can be rehearsed in front of the mirror. As we saw in the practical task above, there is also great value in actually scripting key passages of the lesson to help you improve your vocal delivery in terms of your technical skills.

- Imagining responses to various different scenarios and planning courses of action. These need not be extreme situations. It may be something as simple as a pupil asking an awkward or seemingly irrelevant question. Having a number of good diversion or re-focussing statements up your sleeve can smooth over potentially problematic exchanges.

- Rehearse a few jokes! There is a significant amount of literature that emphasises the importance of humour in creating positive learning and teaching environments (Garner 2005; Hill 1988). Whilst we may not all be natural wits, there is plenty of time to rehearse and practise a few, relevant jokes to insert with your lesson plan. Pupils will really enjoy this element if it is done well. We will consider this further in Chapter 5.

Make time for reflection

Our thesaurus (Collins 2002) has following entry for 'reflection': 'a calm, lengthy, intent consideration'; it follows this with words such as 'musing, rumination, thoughtfulness, contemplation, reflection, meditation, introspection and speculation'.

In the hurly-burly of school life, you might ask yourself whether reflection, whilst desirable, is possible! Many programmes of initial teacher education are built around the idea of the 'reflective practitioner'. But how realistic is an approach to teaching as a reflective practice for every teacher?

We would argue that reflection is an essential type of activity for all teachers to undertake. This is true throughout your whole career, but it could be especially important during moments of transition (e.g. when you are coming into teaching, when you are moving between jobs or taking on a new role).

So, what does it mean to be a reflective teacher? Drawing on the work of Donald Schön (Schön 1983, pp. 332–334), we think it involves the following.

The reflective teacher:

- Listens to their students and really seeks to understand them as unique individuals, tailoring their instruction, speech and learning resources to respond to their specific requirements;

- Thinks beyond their lesson plan in seeking to respond to individual students' needs and requirements;

- Uses the curriculum as an inventory of themes to be understood rather than a set of materials to be learnt;

- Expands their knowledge of the students to encompass their learning and interests outside of the classroom;

- Uses technology in a way to empower students to undertake their own learning rather than to reinforce old-fashioned, teacher-centric pedagogies;

- Prioritises independent, qualitative, narrative accounts of learning over blunt, accountability-driven assessment frameworks that depersonalise the student and their achievements;

- Challenges set theories of knowledge and its organisation within the school systems of timetables and classrooms, seeking to make links in imaginative ways across and in-between subject boundaries.

This is quite a challenge! But do not be daunted. Reflective practice can start simply and quietly, in your own mind or in a private teaching journal. It need not be part of a grand scale process of performance management or other accountability mechanisms. In fact, it would be better to kept out of these frameworks. We think it too important to be compromised by them.

But, you might argue, the general business of school life can compromise any well meaning approach to develop a reflective practice. Clearly, this is a danger. But the writers on reflective practice recognise this and, more importantly, identify the larger structural forces at work in any organisation that can compromise an individual's attempt to be reflective. Here, for example, is Schön writing about how the structure of many educational systems works against reflective practice. He asks us to imagine a school whose work is characterised by a range of features (some of which you may recognise). It is:

- Built around a theory of knowledge that dictates that it is the teacher's job to teach and students to learn. Knowledge is imparted by teachers in 'measurable doses', with students digesting these chunks and teachers planning for students' progressive development;

- Orderly, in terms of space and time. It has self-contained classrooms and a regular timetable through which knowledge bases (subjects) are partitioned and delivered;

- Controlled by systems of sanctions and rewards for students, with expectations for individual students set and checked regularly;

- Controlled by systems of sanction and rewards for staff, with management structures ensuring standards are maintained;

- Characterised by objectivity, with quantitative measures of proficiency and progress preferred to qualitative or narrative accounts of learning and teaching.

As you read through this list, perhaps you recognised some of these features from the schools that you have visited or worked within? The bureaucratic model of schooling he outlines imposes significant restraints on the work of the aspiring reflective teacher. However, it need not quash it completely. Part of working through a process of reflective practice is understanding the forces that can mitigate against it.

So, how can you respond as a teacher?

1. Make a firm commitment to practise the art of being a reflective teacher.

2. Find a short period of time each day, even if it is just a few minutes, to reflect on the teaching you have engaged with during the day. Ask yourself simple questions like:

3. What went well?

4. What did not go so well?

5. How could you improve things?

6. What would you do differently next time?

7. Keep a teaching journal, if not all the time at least for a set or specific period (e.g. whilst you are considering the introduction of a new style of vocal delivery) to help you reflect more deeply on that specific issue.

8. If possible, find a colleague to help share your reflections and act as a 'critical friend'.

This kind of reflective practice can be really helpful when you are considering something as personal as developing your voice in new directions within your teaching. In order to do this well, it is important to really think hard about what excellence in teaching looks and sounds like. To help us with this, we are going to consider the work of one of the leading proponents of 'artistry in teaching', Elliot Eisner.

The final part of this chapter seeks to challenge your notion of what exactly a teaching identity might be. It does this by considering a metaphor and applying this to the act of teaching.

Elliot Eisner was the Professor of Education and Art at the University of Stanford. He made an invaluable contribution to the world of art and education in various ways, not least through his expositions of the artistry of teaching. Artistry, Eisner argues, has much to teach the world of education:

> Artistry, therefore, can serve as a regulative ideal for education, a vision that adumbrates what really matters in schools. To conceive of students as artists who do their art in science, in the arts, or the humanities, is, after all, both a daunting and a profound aspiration. It may be that by shifting the paradigm of education reform and teaching from one modelled after the clock-like character of the assembly line into one that is closer to the studio or innovative science laboratory might provide us with a vision that better suits the capacities and the futures of the students we teach. It is in this sense, I believe, that the field of education has much to learn from the arts about the practice of education. It is time to embrace a new model for improving our schools.
>
> (Eisner 1996, p. 18)

Eisner suggests that recognising artistry as teaching gives us a way of seeking out its particular artistic elements and using these to help think, and talk, about teaching in different ways. Eisner gives us some examples. The idea of a teacher as a performer might conjure up images in your mind of an actor or musician delivering a performance of some type. It is worth pausing to consider this in a bit more detail. What makes for a convincing dramatic or musical performance? What are the features that might make it compelling or engaging? How does the performer present or shape the music or words in an expressive way to communicate their thoughts or emotions at particular moments? All of these questions could be applied and developed to help you consider your vocal delivery as a teacher.

Eisner relates artistry to the processes of criticism and reflection. He talks about specific aspects of feedback that teachers receive about their work. He draws on the ideas behind artistic criticism which aims towards a re-education of the perception of the work of art. Eisner's application of his teaching as artistry metaphor urges us to rediscover a form of educational criticism, characterised by sensitive observations and interpretations of our teaching which reflect the particular context of our work. As we were discussing above, your ability to reflect deeply on your own teaching practice can be one of the deepest forms of productive self-criticism.

Viewing teaching as artistry will allow us to also become more tolerant of how other teachers teach. Eisner has an aversion to bureaucracies and standardisation of processes of teacher development. For example, substitute the word 'teaching' for 'artistry' in the following paragraph:

> Artistry courts surprise. It welcomes initiative. It celebrates imagination. . . . Artistry acknowledged and prized might encourage teachers to make their professional lives interesting by thinking of themselves as being engaged in the practice of an art.
>
> (ibid.)

The types of questions that we can draw from these sentences to our own teaching are very challenging:

- How often does my teaching surprise my students? Does it even surprise me?

- How does my teaching celebrate the imaginative and respond positively to new initiatives or approaches?

- How much time do I spend seeking out the experimental and new approaches that might help me conceive of what I do as a teacher in terms of being an artist?

- Do I respond appropriately when my pupils show these attributes in their work?

- To what extent do I value uniformity in my teaching approach? Can I really allow for the differences in pupils' learning that might occur if losing the reins of a structured and systematic (mechanistic) approach to the development of my teaching?

Finally, conceiving of teaching as artistry will lead, Eisner believes, to the creation of a profession where there is less tolerance for simplified (perhaps we might say 'top-down') solutions to educational problems. Rather, the notion of teaching as an art will lead to a greater degree of complexity because it emphasises the individual identity of the teacher and prioritises the subtleties that they will exhibit through their artistic, teaching practice. In this sense, one size does not fit all. In Eisner's terms, it 'invites risk, courts challenge, and fosters growth' (ibid.).

Eisner's work is a challenge to all teachers. For those of us who have been teaching for longer it will be harder to break free from old, restricting habits and pedagogies. For those of you starting out at the beginning of your teaching careers, we would urge you to consider the key messages of this chapter very carefully. Start as you mean to go on. Use Peshkin's work that we considered in Chapter 1 to help provide yourself with a greater understanding of your identity and how it applies to your work as a teacher. Respond positively to Schön's call for reflective practitioners. Although schools can be very bureaucratic places, there is room for individuality, talent and flair. This can be exhibited in your vocal delivery alongside the wider aspects of your pedagogy. Eisner's concept of teaching as artistry can empower you to break out of mechanistic models of teaching, pinned down by external curriculum requirements or approaches, and allow you to develop your pedagogy in such a way that celebrates life in its fullness and inspires your pupils to do the same.

References

Collins (2002) *Thesaurus of the English Language: Complete and unabridged 2nd edition*. New York: HarperCollins Publishers.

Curran, A. (2008) *The Little Book of Big Stuff about the Brain*. Carmarthen: Crown House Publishing Ltd.

Eisner, E. (1996) 'Is "The art of teaching" a metaphor?'. In Kompf, M., Bond, W. R., Dworet, D. and Boak, R. T. (eds) *Changing Research and Practice: Teachers' professionalism, identities and knowledge*. London: Falmer Press.

Garner, R. (2005) 'Humor, analogy, and metaphor: H.A.M. it up in teaching'. *Radical Pedagogy* 6:2. Also available from: http://radicalpedagogy.icaap.org/content/issue6_2/garner.html [last accessed 14/1/17].

Hill, D. (1988) *Humor in the Classroom: A handbook for teachers*. Springfield, Il: Charles C. Thomas.

Quirke, A. (2017) 'Eight things Richard Burton did to acquire "that" voice'. http://www.bbc.co.uk/programmes/articles/bMmjjHMnRknJGv8NcXJhxZ/eight-things-richard-burton-did-to-acquire-that-voice [last accessed 3/3/17].

Salter, J. (2005) 'Final word'. *Report* July/August, p. 30. London: Association of Teachers and Lecturers.

Schön, D. (1983) *The Reflective Practitioner: How professionals think in action*. New York: Basic Books.

Shirley, D. (2017) 'Effective public speaking: Notes for guidance'. Manchester: Manchester Metropolitan University (unpublished).

Chapter 4

Your voice and your body language

ICONIC VOICE PORTRAITS

Chris Evans is an English presenter, journalist, producer and business-man. Like many in the popular media he has had many up and downs both professionally and personally. He can be equally liked and disliked by many for his antics, work and life.

His voice has been key to his success, though. Although not renowned for having a great voice like many of the 'iconic voices' you will discover throughout the chapters, Chris Evans is a brilliant example of an 'interesting' voice. So, what is interesting about his vocal delivery?

Chris is not especially known for having a 'big' voice; there isn't lots of air going through it. This is probably the first reason why this is especially well suited to television or radio. The amplification or broadcast technologies will 'do' that part of the work.

Second, Evans uses his natural pitch very well. He doesn't vary it a great amount, which makes him 'easy' to listen to. This is also a great example that to have an interesting voice doesn't mean changing your voice a great amount. If you listen to early and later recordings of Chris' voice there isn't a great change.

His use of pace and clarity are especially good, though. He is excellent at using this to change mood, to show excitement, to draw you in but the clarity of what he is saying is rarely lost. This is a fabulous thing to have when speaking on radio.

Perhaps most important though, is that he has the ability to show real passion, fun and enthusiasm for what he does through his voice. He is not afraid to let go to show his exuberance and excitement for the task at hand.

It is worth listening to his voice and asking why it is so engaging. What is it about its clarity, unity of pitch and emotion that helps the listener to be drawn in by it?

It is clear, over time, that his voice has been key to his success.

There is no mystery to body language; everybody assesses body language everyday.

(Peters 2012, p. 170)

Following on from our discussions about your voice and vocal delivery in Chapter 3, this chapter will explore how your voice and body language work together within the classroom. Key teaching scenarios will be explored to demonstrate how an effective teaching voice works in conjunction with your body language to create a strong teaching identity. This has many applications. One of the most common applications will be to help you create a behaviour management strategy that is positive and affirming and not negative and confrontational.

There is much research to suggest that body language is one of the primary functions that our brain assesses continually for our survival. Even in the arguably simpler brains of our pets and animals, it is clear that they react very quickly to changes in body language and nonverbal forms of communication compared with voice and words.

In Chapter 3 we considered the work of Andrew Curran, a leading consultant paediatric neurologist working at Alder Hey Children's Hospital. He presents the idea that the primary function of our brain is to keep us alive. This makes sense as without this we have no other functions we can build upon. Thus our brain, even without us knowing it, is scanning each move that everyone around us makes to assess whether we are safe or not, whether there is a chance for an 'attack' and whether we need to defend ourselves in some way.

In his book, Peters (2012) suggests that it is our 'chimp' part of our brain that does this without our 'human brain' even knowing:

Body language is simply the term used for a message that we convey without speaking. Instead of speaking we use facial expression, positioning and movement of our body.

(Peters 2012, pp. 170–171)

He goes on to explore 'the presentation and packaging of communication' that are shown in four different ways in our human communication:

- Body language;

- Intonation;

- Use of word;

- Ambience.

Amy Cuddy, a Professor at Harvard Business School, is a social scientist and in her TED talk in 2012 focussed on body language or, as she defines it, 'non verbal communication' (Cuddy 2012). Learning to read the language of your own body and that of others is an inextricable part of how we communicate together. Just as in the way that all of our interactions in life shape our brain, its functions, our ways of thinking, our body language shapes who we are. For us, it seems logical that as we explore the productive use of the voice in the classroom and an associated pedagogy, our body language is another integral factor to consider.

Right from our earliest years, we learn to watch others. Anyone who has enjoyed the company of a newborn, will know the excitement when their eyes open for the first time and visual contact is made. No doubt it is a bit blurry for a few weeks, but eventually babies learn to control their gaze and can recognise the faces of parents and siblings and show signs of recognition. It is an *amazing* moment for all. Moving from that point forwards, you become an expert at reading the body language of others. It is one of the primary ways that we make first decisions about people, decide who we will like or dislike and who we will develop initial friendships with. We develop an understanding of personal space and begin to understand how we accept others into our space.

Before you read further into this it might be worth considering whether you have ever thought about your use of body language as a *tool*. By this, we mean something that you choose to use for a particular situation or task. Do you match certain nonverbal tools with particular work or life tasks?

Our first direct consideration of body language was introduced to us at secondary school when we had to do mock college and work interviews. We were introduced to the idea of nonverbal communication with some basics of how to sit, maintain eye contact and not fidget. Will's main memory from this was a list of 'things' he shouldn't do rather than a positive introduction to body language as a useful tool.

Peters (2012) gives us some clear examples of body language that we may have also experienced at some point:

> If we *tower over someone* when talking to them, most people would find this very intimidating and threatening and any message offered might get interpreted with a negative feeling attached to it. It is the same as having your body space invaded. We all have a space around us that we feel belongs to us and if someone gets too close and is unwelcome then we immediately feel uncomfortable. Body space is different from culture to culture and person to person but the general rule is that we are programmed to feel comfortable as arm's length from one another. Any closer leaves us uneasy unless we are welcoming to it.
>
> *Crossing our arms* generally means that we feel attacked and are being defensive. It can also mean that we are being overloaded with information or are not sure we want the information being given.
>
> (Peters 2012, p. 171)

Peters offers the concept that we can consider body language and the leverage that we can have upon others by the use of it. The facts seem to be that your brain is considering at all times the body language of others so it might be better to more consciously consider at times 'What is your body saying to me? What is my body language saying to you?' (Cuddy, 2012).

We can all recount times when we have taken a disliking for someone who we have only just met or have even only encountered from the far side of a room at a party, conference or other social gathering. Anecdotally, Will knows that more often than not it is his wife who uses this as a very primary way of considering whether she will be friends with someone or be willing to listen to their advice or delivery. Some researchers and writers would suggest that this is clearly modelled in the animal kingdom but may not be as evident in modern humans.

Harari, Peters and others certainly touch on the idea of this importance in the animal world. The male species in many more combative animals are often much stronger, physically superior and loaded with more testosterone. It is therefore going to be key for survival that the females in the group are adept and educated in the reading of nonverbals and able to react quickly to them. As an aside, Will's wife would certainly argue that her reading of body language is far more developed than his (but don't read too much into this!).

These nonverbal forms of communication are also evident in photographs and videos that we capture and share through our social media. Some psychologists believe that there is only going to be a significant development in our abilities to communicate nonverbally as these ways of interacting take precedence over real time, spoken work communication.

Power in human body language is often linked to:

- An open, strong, upright body position;

- Arms being raised or open;

- Gestures being used to accompany language, e.g. hands are used to support talk;

- Lots of handshakes are offered;

- Dominating an area and moving around it in a proactive manner;

- Using lots of positive eye contact.

Cuddy (2012) gives the example of the gesture athletes adopt when winning a race, i.e. that of throwing your arms aloft in celebration (not one that Jonathan has experienced very often). This has been shown to be done by blind as well as sighted athletes.

A virtually opposite list could be made for signs of weakness, lack of power or disinterest. It is going to be interesting to develop your own understanding of how your body language has shaped your teaching and communication so far both positively and negatively. It is likely as an experienced teacher that you may have already developed many positive uses of your body without even realising it.

As human beings we are influenced in making decisions, in engagement and learning by many things including nonverbal communication. As a teacher you may have already considered what your students' body language is telling you. As an observer in a classroom these are often very easy to see. Some of the more negative forms of body language or nonverbal communication that can be seen regularly (but never in your classroom we hope!) include students:

- With their heads down or gazing out of a window;

- Fidgeting or playing with small objects like pens or rulers;

- Picking at clothes, uniform, nails or skin;

- Writing or doodling patterns;

- Slumped in their chairs or swinging around on them precariously!

As we busy ourselves with the complexities of teaching though, especially earlier in our career where more energy goes into the act of teaching, we can so often miss much of this. It is very similar to when we begin to drive. There seems so much to do with the clutch, brake, accelerator, indicators that we have no time to just look out of the window and see the scenery we are passing. We might just as well be driving down a computer image grey street, hopefully noticing potential hazards but little more.

Inexperienced or poor teachers are very similar with nonverbal communication. They are so busy teaching and focussing on what they need to do or how they need to communicate that they struggle to read even the most obvious forms of body language. It is a vital part of classroom management that you consider what your body language says to students and what your students' nonverbal language tells you about their engagement.

Even though the worry of most people training to teach will be 'What do I do if they all hate me?', and 'How do I deal with hecklers or students who shout out?', what could be worse than being faced by rows of blank-faced students, the ones whose body language says entertain me, educate me, engage me even though I have already decided that I'm going to try and exclude myself from your classroom whilst still being here?

Mind and body

We have mentioned in other chapters the importance of how we learn. How the chemicals in your brain and body need to be balanced to allow real learning to take place. But before moving onto the more practical aspects of body language and voice and how we can develop a positive approach in the classroom, we need to consider the relationship between mind and body.

In the opening part of the chapter we have explored how we read and are influenced by body language. But how does our body language affect us in the opposite way? If our body language influences how others think about us, how does our body language affect our own minds, our social interactions and the development of skills?

Cuddy's research (Cuddy 2012) has explored the balance of cortisol and testosterone in a selection of candidates who exhibited strong and assertive body language. Cortisol is a steroid hormone that is released in the body as a reaction to stress, anxiety or worry. Testosterone is the primary male sex hormone. It is associated with power and dominance. The initial findings of her research found that dominant, confident people are more likely to smile, more likely to gamble and think they will win, and generally be positive about situations.

She went on to design research to look at the balance of hormones and whether this is affected by short and clear acts of body movement. She had observed that the more powerful people exhibited certain nonverbal characteristics, but wanted to explore whether the nonverbal characteristics actually change their minds in terms of the balance of cortisol and testosterone.

It is worth watching her TED Talk and seeing the evidence for yourself. It might even stimulate further enquiry or research. What is important for us here is to realise that there is a clear two-way effect between our body language and our minds. In Cuddy's words, 'our bodies change our minds, not just our minds change our bodies' (ibid.).

However, Cuddy's theory goes further than this. She posits the notion that even faking types of open or closed, powerful or weak postures will have an effect on our development, hormones, thinking and social interactions. Her principle that seems highly relevant to our discussion about the development of positive body language within the classroom is this, 'we must **fake it till we make it, or fake it 'til we are it'** (ibid.). In other words, you may not feel like a powerful, awe-inspiring teacher every day, but even acting as though you are one will have a positive impact on your mind and body, on how you think and how you act in the classroom. You might have to fake it for a while, but eventually this in and of itself has a positive impact on your thinking and actions as a teacher. This is vitally important!

In our careers so far we have taught in the classroom for some ten years and in a university, training teachers, for 16 years. On occasions, we still get a feeling that someone might come along and tap us on the shoulder and tell us that we're not doing this very well, that we're just messing about and enjoying teaching, and that the university ought to employ someone who really has the skills to do the job! We think this is probably quite a natural state of affairs for most teachers, primarily because:

1. Our development as teachers is not a set acquisition of skills. To be a good or effective teacher is not a single thing. To be a good teacher we need to be reflective, self critical and forever learning. So, if we ever felt like we had made it or achieved it perhaps it would be time to give up?

2. We do something that we love, that we are passionate about, that we are immersed in. Therefore, in one sense it never seems like work, it never seems too difficult to overcome new challenges;

3. We learn as much from the students we teach each year as they learn from us. Possibly more. The ideas we collect seeing them teach, working and developing constantly inspires new thinking, skills and ideas in us too.

Whether we are faking or not, the important thing is that we are doing the job and trying our hardest to do it well. This will have positive consequences for ourselves and our students.

In considering these things, it is important to start to plan for small improvements. Small tweaks can make big changes. Start to consider how you can prepare each day, before each lesson and build your understanding of your body language into this.

In the end, you are how you sound! Your students will see you often before they hear you. So, what does this mean for the way that you will act every day of your teaching career?

The tools of teaching

Teaching is a vocally demanding and energetic profession. It demands long periods of speaking in environments that are detrimental for your voice. You will be competing for students' attention in environments that are often poorly ventilated and acoustically challenging. There are few opportunities for rest built into your timetable. If you add in the additional demands of meetings, tutorials, break time duties, parent–teacher meetings, student reviews and the like you will have little time left for just having a chat in the staffroom.

It may seem obvious, but teachers of all ages, in all countries and in many different settings, are one of the largest groups of professional voice users each day. Despite this, vocal coaching or training is rarely included as part of a teacher's professional training. The consequences of this for vocal health are dire (and we'll explore these further in Chapter 8). Although many teaching courses will contain elements of training around how to use your voice productively, few approach the topic in anywhere near enough detail to make a significant difference to how teachers sound day by day, week by week and year by year. However, it is our contention that this needs to change, not just so that you can enjoy a long and productive teaching career with a healthy voice, but also so your students can benefit from you being the best and most inspiring teacher that you can be!

Your body language and your voice are essential tools in your teaching. As important as the lesson plan, the teaching activities, the resources and the learning that will flow from these, it will be your communication, your body language and voice, which will help shape your teaching. Every lesson!

Crucially, our view is that your body language in the classroom creates around 80 per cent of your total visible identity as a teacher. Think about this from your students' point of view. If 80 per cent of what you are communicating is about your body language it is, perhaps, time that we gave this more attention.

This is not to say that good teachers don't have good body language. But as you will discover (if you haven't done so already), the energy that goes into lesson planning, marking, monitoring progress and countless other tasks working outside of the classroom, could be getting wasted by your lack of focus on effective communication within the classroom. Think about your body language in the classroom as a mirror that reflects your self-confidence as a teacher, your health, age, emotion and mood.

As with your voice, you need to consider how you look after your whole body. Your voice depends on it. In the end, it is the most expensive instrument in the world. Your body adds meaning to all of your vocal communication. The position of your body and its use directly affects the pitch, rate, dynamic and size of your voice.

In an average teaching day, thinking about the huge range of things that you try to do with your voice:

■ You talk extensively;

■ You talk loudly;

■ You speak over classroom noise and other background sounds;

■ You need to fill a large teaching space, even competing with other teachers in some of the large teaching spaces of new schools;

■ You communicate subtle ideas over large distances;

■ You use your voice to control student behaviour in close proximity and from afar.

Yet, most teachers we know do not start their days with any physical or vocal warm ups! Your voice is key for classroom instruction, to maintain discipline and focus, to communicate tasks, to provide encouragement and support students' work.

So, it is essential that you consider how you can better support your professional tools, that is your voice and your body language, to support your teaching on a daily basis. How you use these tools on a daily basis will shape your pedagogy. Here's one simple example, music teachers who are teaching six classes in a day won't plan to sing with each class. This would put far too much strain on their bodies and voices.

PRACTICAL TASK

List the main activities of your classroom and consider how often these activities are used. Now consider what effort this places on your voice and body during the day.

Is it necessary? Are there other ways that lessons could be planned and delivered that may help your communication but crucially vary the pressure placed upon your voice?

Addressing the professional standards for teaching

As touched on earlier in this chapter, the use of voice and even less so body language are often not focussed on during your training year as a teacher. Like many professions today, there is a continued focus on the measurable elements of the work we do rather than the key skills that underpin these. In the United Kingdom we have the professional standards for teaching that underpin the work of all teacher training courses and provide a focus for judgement made about you and your early work as a teacher.

Sadly, within the professional standards for teaching there is no mention of the voice or body language. So, let's consider for a moment how the teaching standards could be supported, influenced and developed by considering the importance of your communication, both verbal and nonverbal.

A teacher must:

Set high expectations that inspire, motivate and challenge pupils

- establish a safe and stimulating environment for pupils, rooted in mutual respect

- set goals that stretch and challenge pupils of all backgrounds, abilities and dispositions

- demonstrate consistently the positive attitudes, values and behaviour which are expected of pupils.

(DfE, 2015)

How much of this will be influenced by body language and voice but more importantly how can you work on this? Even if we consider the tasks, rules, goals, demonstrations we can plan and execute how much of these will be supported by our effective, or not effective, communication.

Developing good body language is not something that is easy to do, though. It will take time, critical reflection and willingness to work on things to change. One of the great positives, though, is that it can be easily practised without a class. The first part of this is in being comfortable in yourself and becoming comfortable in your teaching environment.

It is crucial to 'own' the teaching space. Even experienced teachers will benefit from checking a space before teaching in it. Here's a quick checklist:

- How big is the space?

- How many areas can I easily access to teach from?

- Are there any outside or background noises that it will be useful to be aware of? This might even mean considering whether the grass is being mown outside during summer.

- What influence do I have in changing any of this space to make it better support my use of body and voice?

Most importantly though, take some time to know the space, to relax into it and develop positive body language that supports you and makes you feel 'at home' in that space. If the teaching space isn't the most supportive of environments due to factors outside of your control how can you change this?

It can help to observe other teachers in that space and similar areas and focus on the use of body language and verbal communication. Could you make a list of a few things that you could consider developing in your teaching or has it made you aware of areas you need to develop or eradicate. At this time don't be afraid to 'try things'. Teaching is about experimenting and trying new ideas even when the ones you have are successful. This continued self evaluation and development will help you keep your work fresh over many years.

It is key for student teachers to acknowledge, though, that experienced professionals in walks of life make the difficult things look easy. There are so many subtle changes of body language, position in the room, a fleeting glance to 'that pupil' before an experienced teacher even talks that can so easily and obviously be missed. This is often most true when trainee teachers first try to copy the model of teaching they have been observing, with far less effective control and communication. Preparing in the space and considering body language will help you more quickly along the path of developing effective classroom communication.

In our experience, most trainee teachers have an energy and willingness to experiment and this is a good starting point. Let's consider three main tasks that might arise in an average teaching day:

1. Starting the lesson, getting control and focus as the students enter, settle and prepare for work.

2. Communicating the main task and the focus for the lesson or activities that will be covered.

3. A whole class intervention part-way through the main task to ensure progress is being made over time, standards are high and students are completing work as they should.

Let's develop a few questions around the body language and voice needed for each of them in turn.

1. Where should or could the teacher be at the start of the lesson? What 'sort of voice' will be needed? How can body language positively support the start of the lesson? Consider making a few varied observations of teachers in lessons to further develop your ideas.

2. Now onto communicating, modelling or using questions to set the main task. How should the body language and voice change now? What do you need your voice and body to convey to the students? How can you draw them into the task and make them want to do it? A key part of learning and the brain is the 'what's in for me' question that students are considering in this moment. Is your body and voice ready to convey what's in it for them? Have you planned not just what you'll do but how you'll do it?

3. The whole class intervention. What voice will be needed to get the attention of the class and how will it then need to change? What will you tell the students, what will you ask? What is the reason or focus for the intervention? Where will you be in the room? What will your body language be like? What vocal range will you need to consider to do this most effectively?

In our experience it seems that although body language and voice are linked and so important to even these three activities, it is rarely considered as part of the training you will receive. Copying an established teacher will only get you so far. But finding your own teaching identity, with your own sound and 'look', is a longer journey that you need to commit to undertake.

From our observations, we often find that younger teachers fall into the trap of a mono-dimensional approach to the voice. This can be quite a constant, relatively high pitch, semi-shout that will vary very little in pitch, speed or size. Would you want to listen to this? What effect does it have on your body and voice health? What effect does this have on the students? Will they want to listen? While reading about any of the 'iconic voices' in each chapter of the book are any of them described in a way that mirrors this? No.

This poor communication can often result in an ever-decreasing circle of negative student behaviour. If your nonverbal and verbal communication are poor anyway, how are you going to deal with this? You will probably communicate in a way that is even more negative in its use of your voice and body. You are more likely to quickly move into shouting or communicating in a way where very few students are listening.

You may be advised to wait for silence. On its own this is not bad advice but what body language will you need when waiting for silence, what sort of nonverbal communication might be effective? If you don't get that right you might be waiting at the front of the classroom for a very long time!

More positively, observing, practising and modifying body language, including positioning in a room relative to others, can have many positive outcomes. Varying the voice and body language together can help in many ways:

- Better communication. Better listening, better teaching. This can be even more important with younger pupils and SEN or bilingual learners.

- It will help you to relax, which will give you a 'better body' for communication, thus a better sound, less stress in voice and in teaching/classroom.

- It will all help with your emotional health.

Emotional health and well being

It is hopefully becoming clear that better use of your voice and your body will help you better balance the use of your energy during the day. The cumulative effect of having a 'better day' will feedback into you feeling better generally about your work, your relationships and your wider life too. The science supports the importance of a healthy body and a healthy mind in all aspects of communication.

An obvious way to maximise your emotional health is to work on reducing the stress levels associated with work and your life outside of work. Thinking more about time to rest your voice, planning your teaching day differently and thinking about communication as a whole will have positive influences on your wellbeing.

Seeking help, reading or talking with others may be a vital part of this. Like in all elements of teaching, many of the answers are not within yourself. There are many ways to reduce stress and negative emotions and it could start with some of the following simple steps:

- Thinking about diet. Do you eat food that supports the energy you need? Do you miss meals and grab sugary snacks that might give you spikes of energy during the day, but contribute little to sustained work and relaxed mood?

- Do you drink enough water? This is vital for voice and energy. Coffee, the mainstay of many teachers' days, is well proven to affect the voice badly. Again, what effect do spikes of caffeine have during the day?

▓ Do you plan breaks for your voice and body? Where you can sit for two minutes in a positive way to collect your thoughts and move forwards productively?

▓ Do you plan a small amount of exercise to give yourself time to think and relax?

Working with many trainee teachers, it is clear that learning to teach is a very stressful time. It is not just about workload, but also the long days, unrelenting accountability and also the personal challenge.

Your voice and body are key in this. Preparing physically before lessons, preparing how to relax and giving yourself time to be confident will be key. Try to read a little more about how anxiety and emotional health can affect you and your teaching and how you can manage this productively. Right now is a great time to start as you mean to go on, to better understand how your brain works, how you learn and unlearn and how you manage your inner self to better support your life generally and, specifically, your teaching activities.

Failing to do this will lead to stress. Stress alters the voice. It is easy to hear nerves or worry in the voice. It is also easy to see it in your body language and students will be unsettled by this. All teachers can take simple steps to improve their vocal delivery and body language. Here are some thoughts to get you started.

1. Avoid talking in a monotone voice. Try to vary the pitch, speed and dynamic as we discussed in the previous chapters. Try at least three different voices in your teaching:
   - Look at me;
   - Interesting task;
   - Whole group attention.

2. Use pauses and inflections to gain attention and convey a message as opposed to just increasing volume – you will talk faster than you think. This is natural, especially when you start teaching. So, slow down, put in more pauses. Think about talking in clear bullet points and asking questions to give yourself time to think. Remember the exercises that we did in the previous chapter in relating to preparing an explanation. Plan for pauses and longer pauses and notate these in lessons planning materials if you find that helpful.

4. Avoid starting words in a hard, harsh way – don't start lessons by shouting. Where will you go from this? Don't shout about uniform, lining up or other small issues. If you'd just been shouted at would you be ready to learn?

5. Keep your body, and especially the head and face, relaxed – never clench your teeth or jaw to speak. Your lips are important in shaping the sounds, especially when speaking in a large space or with a big group. You should move your lips a lot to shape words. If you do need to raise your voice in volume just for a moment

still keep the body, neck and head relaxed. Avoid pushing your head forward whilst raising your voice.

6. Practise using your voice in a relaxed manner. Go into classrooms before and after school to practise. Video yourself and try different sounds, body position and posture. Remember the lessons from Chapter 2. Whilst breathing, air (fuel), voice box (phonation) and resonance are the basic building blocks of the voice, the effectiveness of our voices is also affected by your overall relaxation of your body. Remember, it may take time in such a stressful situation to feel relaxed, but the benefits to you and your teaching will be quite measurable. Relaxation of the muscles of the head and in the neck area will have most influence on the voice. Good breathing and practising exercises for this will not only support better voice but also support a more relaxed body.

Body language and posture

A good posture is vital for our vocal delivery and body language. This is because the parts of the body that contribute to voice production are connected to many other parts of the body. The way in which we align our bodies and the amount of muscle tension or relaxation within it will influence the voice because of the links in our muscular and skeletal systems. Excess tension in the muscles of the larynx, for example, can lead to a strained, harsh voice. Tension in any muscles, often the shoulders, will result in some pain. This is a sign that the muscles are not getting a chance to relax as they naturally should. Similarly, standing with your shoulders rounded and the head jutted forward from the spine can lead to difficulty in coordinating relaxed breathing with voice.

What is good posture? Good posture is about using and working with your body. For us, this begins and ends with breathing. You need to work with your posture and breathing to improve it, not try to fix yourself by acting in a new way.

Do consider your posture in the classroom. Do you get any repeated strains, aches or problems? Could your posture be contributing to this? Talk to other teachers. Are there common problems that you could share remedies or ideas about? Consider how your body is used in the 'act of teaching'. For example, do you:

■ Write or type and talk? How do you do this?

■ Fold your arms whilst talking? What impact does this have on your shoulders?

■ Lower your head or twist your neck whilst talking?

Remember that poor posture will create tension in muscles over time. This tension will impact your body and your voice. Start by thinking of a few ways you can support your teaching, body position and communication. Here are some tips to get your started.

1. Preparation is key. Warm the body up for work. Try to take small amount of time to stretch.

2. Be aware of your balance. Take a few moments to stand and sense your weight and balance through your body and feet. Move your weight onto each foot in turn, rock backwards and forwards. Try to sense when you feel more balanced and do this when teaching.

3. Align the head with your spine (ears over shoulders). Try to keep your posture symmetrical. Avoid lowering or twisting the head as much as possible when talking.

4. Keep your arms relaxed. Use them to aid communication, but don't get them 'stuck' in one position.

5. Keep your shoulders level and relaxed and in a slightly forward-sloping position. Practise this to avoid rounding or slouching. Avoid raising your shoulders as this will increase tension and restrict airflow through your voice box.

6. Try to keep your legs relaxed and knee joints loose. Try to direct your feet forward and about shoulder width apart or just narrower. Try to combine this with some easy deep breathing.

7. When speaking to your students, position yourself so that your whole body is facing them (not just your head). Get your students to turn to face you too. This will help their posture and stop them getting fidgety or restless.

8. Try to avoid grabbing parts of your body, folding your arms or fidgeting with badges or hair. This not only sends a negative nonverbal message but increased body tension.

9. No matter what the situation, keep the body as relaxed as much as you can.

Body language and classroom management

It is not our focus here to write extensively about classroom management, what it is and what it isn't. Philosophically, it is important to realise that your voice and body language are as key to managing your classroom as any tips from experienced teachers or school systems. It is important to realise that good classroom management comes from good teaching and reflection. There is no single element that will help you more than another. Don't buy the notion that there is some sort of 'bag of tricks' that teachers can quickly utilise. It doesn't work like that.

Charlie Taylor, who was previously head teacher at the Willows Special School, became a DfE expert adviser on behaviour. In his publication he offers this advice on how to 'get the simple things right':

Behaviour checklist for teachers

Classroom

▓ Know the names and roles of any adults in class;

▓ Meet and greet pupils when they come into the classroom;

▓ Display rules in the class, ensure the pupils and staff know what they are;

▓ Tariff of sanctions displayed in class;

▓ Have a system in place to follow through with all rewards;

▓ Display a tariff of rewards in class;

▓ System in place to follow through with all rewards;

▓ Have a visual timetable on the wall;

▓ Follow the school behaviour policy.

Students

▓ Know the names of children;

▓ Have a plan for children who are likely to misbehave;

▓ Ensure other adults in the class know the plan;

▓ Understand pupils' special needs.

(Taylor 2011, p. 3)

Although this contains some good points and advice this is, for us at least, as useful as listing aspects of how to play tennis well and expecting that by ticking each item in the list that you will win Wimbledon! In all honesty, any teacher will tell you that managing a classroom is a complex art that develops over time. It has more similarities with stand up comedy and dealing with hecklers than ticking a check list.

As we have emphasised throughout this chapter, experts in human behaviour say that 80 per cent of communication relates to your body language. This only leaves 20 per cent being about what you say, or more importantly, how you say it. So, perhaps the lists give us a starting point but learning to use and apply them successfully will be much more important. Posture and body language will directly affect the messages that students take from you. Human brains are programmed to do this. Good posture will support your voice but also convey more convincing messages. Here are some tips:

1. Standing up straight adds power and authority to your voice but also conveys a message about interest, attitude and being in charge in the room. The opposite will happen when you slump, stick out your stomach, swing on one leg or look uncomfortable. Over time this will not only be physically unhealthy but will affect your control. Neither of us can ever remember teaching sitting down.

2. Avoid all sorts of body and physical barriers. Folding your arms, standing behind a desk or hiding behind classroom equipment will send a hidden (or clear) message that you are worried about communication or connecting with the pupils. You need to avoid shuffling any paper, checking your phone or watch. All these send messages of disinterest and create barriers to communication.

3. Consider the classroom space. It may be important to start the lesson from the front to take a register or communicate with the aid of ICT resources but there are always other ways. Make sure you use the whole space, and *plan to do this*. Consider backgrounds but most importantly 'own' the whole space. Be comfortable. The power of standing closer to a pupil who is lacking focus can often be far more effective than any confrontation.

4. Move you face! Your lips are key to form words but your smile is also vital. Be interesting in how you look, your facial expressions tell students a lot about what you are really thinking. They will be experts in reading this without knowing. So use it to your advantage. Make eye contact, focus on students who are talking and deal with individuals but include everyone.

5. As we have been saying throughout this chapter, link body and voice. In the same ways that we have encouraged you to develop at least three clear voices, try to develop body language that goes with these. Make sure your body and tone of voice are saying the same as your words. There is no value in shouting 'I'm sorry!'

6. Keep relaxed. Take your time. Think. Give yourself and your students time to think. The best teachers have a way of delivering the lesson while at the same time observing themselves from above to evaluate themselves on the spot. You need to read the body language of pupils to know when to move on, when to slow down.

It is key to remember that your students are picking up on your body language without knowing it and you are sending messages without knowing it. The art of the teacher is to understand this process better and, over time, to learn to control it too.

Linsin (2009) expands on these ideas, introducing the notion of 'creating leverage' for teachers linked to their presence in the room:

Leverage simply means having great influence with your students. This is where the real power comes from. It explains how a teacher can take over a classroom of students from a tough neighborhood, given up on and deemed uncontrollable, and turn them into a dream class. It's the answer to the question, "How was she able to do that with *those* kids?"

(Linsin 2009)

When you walk into a classroom do the students know that you are there? Do you have that presence? If not, how do you go about getting it? It's important. We agree with Linsin that your positive body language is a key aspect of how much 'leverage' you have in the classroom:

> Think about what your typical body language is communicating to your students and how it's affecting your classroom management success. Is it increasing the amount of leverage you have with your students or is it making it more difficult to influence them?

(ibid.)

Classroom presence is something that will take time to develop; it can even take steps backwards when we take on a new job or class as an experienced teacher. It is something slightly different for each teacher and cannot be something that can be simply copied. You need to develop your own style, delivery and build upon your natural body language, which you have already developed up to this point.

PRACTICAL TASK

Focus on some of the points earlier in the chapter and try to evaluate how they affect your students. Do they react to you differently? Also consider how this positively affects you. Consider how a more positive and assertive body language can make you feel about yourself as a teacher.

Try out some of the following next time you are teaching:

- Use more eye contact;

- Smile more often;

- Stand up straight;

- Allow your students their personal space.

Take note of how differently your students respond to you. We know you'll be pleased. Also, notice how changing your body language affects how *you* feel.

We're certain you will look and feel more attractive and confident, resulting in greater leverage with your students and more effective classroom management.

Body language and students' learning

Students will react and copy the body language that you model. The more relaxed and confident you can stay the more your students will be relaxed and more confident to learn.

One of the biggest mistakes of teachers early in their career can be a lack of understanding of the body language of their pupils. There are, for us, two key factors for this.

First, at the beginning, teaching is difficult. It takes lots of your energy and thinking to remember the lesson plan, all of the things you need to get in, that you need to teach the pupils. Like beginning to drive a car there seems to be lots to do and little time to do anything else. As you become more experienced you have more time to see the scenery out of the window.

Second, even when teachers have the time to read body language it is rarely focussed on. Body language can tell much about how engaged students are in what you are doing, whether you have talked for too long, whether they have enough to do. It is vitally important not to confuse students being quiet with students who are listening.

PRACTICAL TASK

Plan time in lesson to try and read the body language of pupils whilst you have less to do. Ask yourself the following questions:

- What does this tell me about my teaching, my communication and my classroom?

- What does the body language of the pupils tell me about the lesson, the learning, the progress they are making?

- What does the individual body language of a pupil tell me about them?

Just beginning to focus on this can be enough to consider how you can more positively consider this in all of your teaching. In fact, it can often become a short obsession of many to read body language.

Try to consider if there is a regular 'body' language that you get from your pupils. Is this linked to your subject, teaching space, chairs or desks? Or is it linked to your body language and teaching style?

It is worth planning to make subtle changes in all of these things so that you can consider what positive benefits this can have for all.

Finally, try to consider how the body language of students relates to their voice, especially their confidence to use their voice in lessons. One of the first messages that students learn in school is that sitting quietly is better than talking. School is often not about their voice. But how much better could it be for the whole of their lives if they can learn to use and control their voice and body language? Could what you learn about yourself be used as a crucial part of your students' learning moving forwards? In that way, perhaps we'll raise a generation of new young people with a strong voices and bodies ready to take on the challenge of educating the next generation.

References

Cuddy, A. (2012) 'Your body language shapes who you are'. https://www.ted.com/talks/amy_ cuddy_your_body_language_shapes_who_you_are [last accessed 25/3/17].

DfE, (2015) 'Teachers' Standards', https://www.gov.uk/government/uploads/system/uploads/ attachment_data/file/283566/Teachers_standard_information.pdf [last accessed 14/3/17].

Linsin, Michael, (2009), 'Body Language and Classroom Management'. https://www.smart classroommanagement.com/2009/09/07/body-language-and-classroom-management/ [last accessed 14/3/17].

Peters, S. (2012) *The Chimp Paradox*. London: Penguin.

Taylor, Charlie (2011) *Behaviour*, Opinion Piece resource, published by the National College for School Leadership, https://www.nationalcollege.org.uk/cm-mc-lit-behaviour.pdf [last accessed 14/3/17].

Chapter 5

What to say and how to say it

ICONIC VOICE PORTRAITS

Mr Reed was a geography teacher at Debenham High School in Suffolk during the 1980s and 1990s. During the later part of that time, Jonathan also taught music at the school.

Mr Reed had an iconic teaching voice. He was an old-fashioned Suffolk gentleman, with a broad Suffolk dialect and a great ability for public speaking, a craft he had honed not just through his teaching but also through his preaching as Methodist lay minister in local churches.

Each school day began with a morning assembly. Following a hymn, which Jonathan led (it was a Church of England school), there was a short talk normally given by the head teacher. Whilst staff were meant to attend these morning assemblies, many would find excuses not to; unless Mr Reed was speaking.

Mr Reed had the most brilliant approach to storytelling. His sense of humour was dry and subtle, but that, together with his broad Suffolk dialect, and his ability to take the audience on a journey with his stories drew students and staff together without fail. It was standing room only! Stories always had a moral that he was able to apply with unerring accuracy to contemporary issues of the day in national, local or school life.

Mr Reed's approach to teaching was definitely 'old school'. You could hear his voice booming out of his geography classroom from the first floor of the main teaching block from pretty much every other part of the school. He didn't suffer fools gladly. That said, Mr Reed had more appreciative letters and visits from ex-students than any other teacher on the staff.

When Jonathan left the school to take up his position at Manchester Metropolitan University, Mr Reed also retired from teaching. Whilst some students got awards for not missing a day of school during the summer term, or the whole year (and, on a rare occasion, for not missing a single day of school at any point during Years 7–11), Mr Reed got an award for not missing a single day of teaching in the various Suffolk schools that he had worked within for over 40 years. That's what we call a long service award!

Mr Reed was loved by students and staff alike. A true character and a gentleman with an iconic voice.

As we considered towards the end of the previous chapter, concepts of reflective practice and artistry in teaching can help us situate the development of our teaching voice in a broader pedagogical context. When we talk about pedagogy, what do we actually mean? Is it as simple as the science of teaching? The main methods of instruction such as explanation, modelling and questioning?

We would argue not. In line with Alexander, we state that:

> Pedagogy is not a mere matter of teaching technique. It is a purposive cultural intervention in individual human development that is deeply saturated with the values and history of the society and community within which it is located. Pedagogy is the act of teaching together with the ideas, values and collective histories that inform, shape and explain that act.
>
> (Alexander 2008, p. 92)

So, our pedagogy provides the broad context within which our ideas about teaching, the shared values that we hold, the forms of practice that we learn to adopt and the tools that we use combine together into the act that we call 'teaching'. Our argument in this book has been that how you speak, and the words that you use, are a core component in your pedagogy. In fact, Alexander would argue that they are the preeminent component in one's pedagogy:

> Of all the tools for cultural and pedagogical intervention in human development and learning, talk is the most pervasive in its use and powerful in its possibilities. Talk vitally mediates the cognitive and cultural spaces between adult and child, among children themselves, between teacher and learning, between society and the individual, between what the child knows and understands and what he or she has yet to know and understand. Language not only manifests thinking but also structures it, and speech shapes the higher mental processes necessary for so much of the learning that takes place, or ought to take place, in school.
>
> (ibid.)

Language is at the heart of learning. Whether written or spoken, whether your voice or your students' voices, the interplay of language mediates learning in fundamental ways. Throughout this book we have been considering how your voice is the tool through which your teaching identity is established in the classroom, and through which your pedagogy is delivered. Alongside this, it is important to consider *what* we say as well as *how* we say it.

As we have seen, the vast majority of teaching involves language, spoken and written. Of course, language is a core component of many human activities and the actions that these activities contain can be analysed. Wertsch's work is particularly helpful to our specific context of language and its use in teaching. Analysis, for Wertsch, allows us to:

> Explicate the relationship between human action, on the one hand, and the cultural, institutional, and historical contexts in which this action occurs, on the other.
>
> (Wertsch 1998, p. 24)

Wertsch calls the link between action and context 'mediated action'. In his book, he gives some examples of mediated action. One of the most famous is pole vaulting.

Pole vaulting has a long history (Rosenbaum 2009), with the first known pole vault competitions being held during the Irish Tailteann Games (dating back as far as 1829 BC). The sport became an Olympic event in 1896. Of course, central to the sport of pole vaulting is the pole! Wertsch uses the pole as an example of how a process of mediated action can be influenced by the tools we choose to use. In the history of pole vaulting, this tool (the pole) and the materials from which it was made have been the source of many problems.

Initially, poles were made of wood. They were probably just large sticks or tree limbs. In the nineteenth century competitors used more refined wooden poles, but these were replaced by bamboo (lighter) poles prior to the Second World War. These poles were lighter and more flexible, allowing the athlete to 'flip' themselves over great heights.

Subsequent developments saw the emergence of metal poles that were stronger but a little less flexible. Today, athletes have the benefit of carbon fibre and fibreglass composite poles (which are lighter, stronger and more flexible). Regardless of the changes in the materials used to make the pole, the aim of pole vaulting has remained the same: to get over the highest possible barrier.

Wertsch's more detailed account of these developments (Wertsch 1998, pp. 27–28) charts the various rivalries and factions within pole vaulting that emerged at the transition points surrounding the adaptation and adoption of new poles. At one point these even included the possibility of breakaway groups favouring a particular type of pole, and accusations that users of new types of poles were cheating. These changes in the sport are documented within the history of pole vaulting itself, which distinguishes between the various 'eras' of particular poles (On Track and Field 2009).

Wertsch's argument is that the pole is essential to pole vaulting. It mediates the action between the athlete (the agent) and the goal of hurtling over the barrier at the highest possible height (the context). His chapter goes onto to explore, through the use of sociocultural analysis and in considerable detail, the relationship between human actions and the cultural, institutional and historical contexts in which this action occurs.

In our context of the classroom, teachers or pupils are the 'agents' (to use Wertsch's terminology), the 'cultural tools' are the objects (physical, virtual, psychological, etc.) we are choosing to use, and the context would be, at least in a simple application of his work, your classroom or other learning spaces where learning occurs. The interplay between agents, tools and contexts is 'mediated action'.

All teaching and learning involves mediated action. Our teaching is mediated by the tools that we choose to use; our pupils' formal and informal learning is mediated by the tools they choose to use. These tools will include our language. The educational goals that we, or our students, establish exist within this wider conceptual framework of mediated action. So, just as you can jump higher within pole vaulting with certain types of poles, you can aim for different educational goals through the effective use of language. Similarly, it may be possible to aim for more challenging, complex teaching and learning if the tools that you have chosen to use take care of basic, lower level functions or issues. The point here is that these tools exist within a wider relationship of teaching, learning and cognitive processes. The teacher's key role will be seeking to exploit the possible educational affordances offered through these relationships.

Wertsch's concept of mediated action allows us to consider our use of the spoken word in a different way. Using Wertch's categorisations, we can define language as being a cultural tool and speech as being a form of mediated action. Drawing on Bakhtin's work, Wertsch exemplifies the spoken word as being a series of 'utterances' that are:

> The real unit of speech communication. Speech can exist in reality only in the form of concrete utterances of individual speaking people, speech subjects. Speech is always cast in the form of an utterance belonging to a particular speaking subject, and outside this form it cannot exist.
>
> (Bakhtin 1986, p. 71)

Utterances are not solely produced by individual speech subjects (that's us!) and unconstrained by other factors. They need to be viewed within a context, or network, of other factors. Some of these are potentially repeatable and others will not be. As he explains:

> Behind each text stands a language system. Everything in the text that is repeated and reproduced, everything repeatable and reproducible, everything that can be given outside a given text (the given) conforms to this language system. But at the same time each text (as an utterance) is individual, unique, and unrepeatable, and herein lies its entire significance (its plan, the purposes for which it was created). This is the aspect of it that pertains to honesty, truth, goodness, beauty, history. With respect to this aspect, everything repeatable and reproducible proves

to be material, a means to an end. This notion extends somewhat beyond the bounds of linguistics or philology. The second aspect (pole) inheres in the text itself, but is revealed only in a particular situation and in a chain of texts (in the speech communication of a given area). This pole is linked not with elements (repeatable) in the system of the language (signs), but with other texts (unrepeatable) by special dialogic relations.

(Bakhtin 1986, p. 105)

According to this theoretical approach, any analysis of the spoken words (utterances) that we make in the classroom context needs to be understood in relationship to the wider language system we are working within (the cultural tool). This will contain important features that implicate the how and what we say as teachers.

Bakhtin's theoretical approach takes things a little further. He introduces the concept of 'speech genres', which are not forms of language per se, but rather are typical 'types' of utterance with a particular kind of expression inherent within them. Bakhtin's view is that speech genres correspond to various different types of situations, e.g. teaching, and that these impact on the style and presentation of utterance as well as the choice and meaning of individual words within this. He continues:

Speech genres organize our speech in almost the same way as grammatical (syntactical) forms do. We learn to cast our speech in generic forms and, when hearing others' speech, we guess its genre from the very first words; we predict a certain length (that is, the approximate length of the speech whole) and a certain compositional structure; we foresee the end; that is, from the very beginning we have a sense of the speech whole, which is only later differentiated during the speech process.

(Bakhtin 1986, pp. 78–79)

Put simply, as we all know from conversations we would have had from our mother's knees, in order to understand someone it is important to listen to not only what they say but how they say it!

Speech genres and utterances within teaching

This quick overview of theory from the work of Wertsch and Bakhtin can help us get to grips with the types of speech that underpin the common types of conversations that we might have with our students each day within our classrooms. It is worth asking what the speech genres that underpin our teaching are.

Defining speech genres is not a precise science. However, we'd like to suggest that there are three main 'types' of speech that teachers routinely use. First, there is what we would call a *whole-school* genre of speech. This is the language that is used to portray a school's ethos, vision and aims. It is something that is used by schools to communicate with students, parents and the local community, particularly in developing aspirations about the school, its function and role. It has a key role in framing school policy and the outworking of this in terms of approaches to school discipline, equal opportunities and other whole school dimensions.

Second, there is a 'generic teaching' speech genre. This concerns the language of instruction, motivation, facilitation and assessment. It is the common framework of ideas that surrounds subjects within the secondary curriculum, their programmes of study, aims and objectives. This speech genre extends across all schools to some extent.

Finally, there are the 'individual subject' speech genres. These are closely related to the whole school and generic teaching speech genres, but are extended and enriched through an individual subject's distinctive language system. Individual subject speech genres draw on the language system of the subject as construed within the educational context, but also from the wider historical and cultural tradition of the subject which have informed that educational context over the years. The individual subject speech genre will contain a range of technical vocabulary, concepts and processes which, whilst drawing on standard language systems, are imbued with significance and meaning that taps into that subject's roots. As we will see in our discussion on metaphors in Chapter 7, unpicking some of this language presents key opportunities for reconstructing teacher and student talk within our classrooms.

This tripartite language framework underpins the 'utterances' that teachers make in the classroom. It informs and mediates not only the choice of words, but also the ways in which these are said and the intentions with which they are imbued. As Bakhtin, in one final quotation, comments:

> There are no "neutral" words and forms – words and forms that can belong to "no one"; language has been completely taken over, shot through with intentions and accents. For any individual consciousness living in it, language is not an abstract system of normative forms but rather a concrete heteroglot conception of the world. All words have the "taste" of a profession, a genre, a tendency, a party, a particular work, a particular person, a generation, an age group, the day and hour. Each word tastes of the context and contexts in which it has lived its socially charged life; all words and forms are populated by intentions.
>
> (Bakhtin 1981, p. 293)

REFLECTIVE TASK

Spend a few minutes reflecting on the various types of language that you use in your classroom. Can you identify the three types of speech genre that have been presented above: whole school, generic teaching and individual subject?

continued

Focus further on the individual subject speech genre. This is likely to dominate large parts of your teaching. What are the subject-based words and forms of speech that you find yourself using? In Bakhtin's words, can you identify elements of the 'taste' of your particular subject in these words or forms of speech? What are the subject's 'intentions' that underlay your utterances? What are the contexts from which these words and forms of speech have derived?

In the following case study, we present a narrative around the changing nature of education in a world of digital technology, with a specific exploration of how music is produced and consumed. Whilst reading it, look out for references, both metaphorical and actual, to language and speech.

CASE STUDY

Teaching and learning in schools is changing dramatically. These changes are part of a much larger social and cultural change driven by many factors, including the use of digital technologies. But the changes go beyond the technological tools themselves. The students have changed as well, maybe not physically but in other important ways. It is hard to overestimate this change. Prensky puts it like this:

> Today's students have not just changed *incrementally* from those of the past, nor simply changed their slang, clothes, body adornments, or styles, as has happened between generations previously. A really big *discontinuity* has taken place. One might even call it a singularity, an event which changes things so fundamentally that there is absolutely no going back. This so-called singularity is the arrival and rapid dissemination of digital technology in the last decades of the twentieth century.
>
> (Prensky 2001, p. 1, his italics)

Prensky draws a useful comparison between those who are 'natives' of this digital revolution and those who are 'immigrants' (Prensky 2001, pp. 2–3). Digital natives are 'native speakers of the digital language of computers, video games and the Internet', whilst digital immigrants have been 'fascinated by and adopted many or most aspects of the new technology but always retain, to some degree, their "accent", that is, their foot in the past' (ibid.). Whilst these distinctions are contentious and have been debated amongst educators (Owen 2006), for the purposes of this study the hypothesis was that 'digital natives'

continued

are working with new technologies in ways far beyond the experience of many 'digital immigrants' who dominate the teaching profession at the current time.

There are numerous examples of this in contemporary society. One major way concerns the way that music is produced, marketed and shared through digital tools and devices. The power of the Internet allows users immediate access to, and purchase of, music from many genres, styles and traditions. Similarly, producers of music exploit the immediate and communicative potential of the Internet to artistically shape their output. Paul Korda, in an interview with Kroeker (2004), stated that:

> File-sharing's effect on music for me, as an artist, is currency. If I record a song today about a current subject, people can hear it tomorrow, given the wide-reaching effects of the Internet. It's the richness of the here and now, bringing new ideas to life, producing them and releasing them to the people. Currency is what technology is all about, and you either move into the future with the here and now, or you live in the past.
>
> (Kroeker 2004)

The price of technologies that allow users to create, perform and share music has fallen so greatly that it is now possible to produce music of extremely high technical quality in the home environment with a modestly equipped personal computer. Indeed, many powerful musical tools that were previously housed within the realm of the professional recording studio are now available freely over the Internet. This has had an impact on the types of spaces that music can be produced within and how this is done. Théberge (1997) has discussed the domestication of the recording studio and indicates that the home studio is essentially a private space both physically (often in a bedroom or basement) and acoustically, with headphones being used as an 'instrument of isolation' (Théberge 1997, p. 234).

These developments continue to move on apace. Yet, the consequences of young people developing their musical skills in this private and isolated world of technologically mediated musical activity for the shared and public world of classroom music has been neglected (Savage 2007).

Prensky's notions of the digital native or immigrant are well known in education and have been rightly challenged by many writers (e.g. Salavuo (2008) questions whether all university students are 'digital natives'). But in relation to our discussion about speech genres and utterances, did you notice the reference to 'accent' in the case study? Prensky used this term to describe the digital immigrant's approach to the use of new technologies. Although they may try hard, according to his theory they cannot shake off the 'accent' of their previous ways of working. Although they have one foot in the present, they also have, in Prensky's terms, one foot in the past that it is impossible to move.

In our earlier analysis of Peshkin's work and his notion of intrinsic subjectivities, we noted that there are core aspects to our psychological make-up that remain us through our lives and that are contextualised within the different situations in which we find ourselves. When we begin teaching, we already have an 'accent' (and we don't mean a regional dialect here) that you will not be able to shake off. It is part of that veil, in Peshkin's terms, that you can't remove. But this is not a negative thing in any way, shape or form! After all, a way of developing a positive approach to language and vocabulary in your teaching should not be about blandness and mediocrity, something that makes all teachers look and sound the same. The preservation of your 'identity' and your 'voice' should remain central at all times.

That said, there are a number of ways that all teachers could usefully develop an approach to utterance that will, when done with respect and sensitivity to one's own identity, school and subject culture, assist in the promotion of effective teaching and learning.

First, let's consider how to develop a consistency with the generic teaching speech genre. In other words, if you are able to use the general language and vocabulary of teaching in a way that builds on students' experience of this in other subjects and areas of the curriculum you will, by default, ensure that your teaching resonates with their wider educational experiences.

As an example, consider the use of the terms 'level' and 'target' in respect of student attainment. Imagine a situation where one teacher talks about 'levels in attainment' in a highly structured way. In fact, they are used so regularly by this teacher that students are told about their progression through sub-levels on an almost weekly basis. When they enter the classroom, there is a large display on the wall showing each of the levels and sub-levels, together with examples of how they can develop their knowledge and understanding from one sub-level to the next. As well as this, as a regular feature of each lesson students receive written feedback from the teacher about their progress, with individual pieces of work being given a sub-level and a target being set for how it can be improved. The use of the words 'level', 'sub-level' and 'target' are an inherent part of this teacher's generic teaching speech genre.

In contrast to this approach, but in the same school, another teacher has a different view about the usefulness of 'levels' and 'targets' within the spoken and written feedback given to students. For this teacher, the 'levels of attainment' are essentially a summative tool, something to be used at the end of each year as a way of reporting back to parents about a student's progress over a longer period. This teacher finds the use of levels, sub-levels and targets as part of the language and vocabulary of an individual lesson is an anathema. Therefore, his choice of language relating to the assessment of individual students is very different. It is more exploratory and, to his mind, less mechanistic. It allows students a greater degree of freedom to grapple with ideas and processes rather than fit within predetermined models of knowledge and how these might be acquired.

Issues relating to assessment are normally contentious. We have used this example not because we want to celebrate one approach and denigrate the other. Rather, we want you to consider what the consequence of this use of language would be for the students who happen to be taught by both teachers. In one sense, this is quite a trite example that concerns a common educational process that all subjects have to adopt in some shape or form. There may be quite valid reasons why assessment is done differently in different subjects. But how does the language that each of these teachers use impact on students' perception of their teachers and the subjects being taught? Are there advantages and disadvantages in terms of the use of written or spoken language and how key messages about progression or assessment are conveyed? To what extent are these messages softened by the type of vocal delivery employed within a specific teaching episode? Should they be softened? There are no easy answers to these questions. But a considered, analytical and reflective approach on your behalf can help you become a teacher with a very skilful and well developed use of language.

Developing classroom talk

At the beginning of this chapter you may recall that we introduced a definition of pedagogy that extended well beyond that associated with teaching skills, tips and tricks. Robin Alexander's broader definition for pedagogy links it to culture in an explicit way. We have built on this in our argument throughout the book that your voice is linked to your teaching identity, and that your teaching identity springs from who you are as a person and, of course, that linked to your genetic makeup and the social interactions that you have experienced throughout your life. We can't divorce these elements from each other. They are all part of you!

For these reasons, the various objectives that are linked to teaching well cannot be achieved through a single method or approach. Don't believe anyone who tells you otherwise. In recent years, certain learning styles or approaches have become popular, often being promoted by large companies looking to make profits out of education. Please steer well clear of these. For clarity, there is no such thing as a kinaesthetic learner. Nor is there an auditory or visual learner either. We are dealing with children in our classrooms, not concepts.

That said, Alexander's work does paint a picture of what the act of teaching looks and sounds like. He does this in his book by considering three 'repertoires for teaching', namely *organisation*, *teaching talk* and *learning talk* (Alexander 2008, pp. 109–110).

In his first repertoire, Alexander describes five key ways in which the organised interactions between you and your students are framed. These will be familiar to anyone who has spent more than a few minutes in a classroom. But, for completeness, here they are:

- Whole class teaching;

- Collective group work (group work led by you);

- Collaborative group work (group work led by students);

- One-to-one activities (in which you work with individual students);

- One-to-one activities (in which students work together in pairs).

As an aside, it is important to note that your selection of the type of organised interaction that you want to adopt within a classroom needs to be chosen carefully and justified in your lesson planning. Clearly, there are many different potential approaches that you could adopt to the teaching of a particular topic, but do make sure that whichever one that you choose to use is chosen for a good reason!

But, more importantly for our discussion here about developing your talk in the classroom, Alexander introduces a second repertoire called *teaching talk*. Drawing on the research data that he collected from an extensive piece of international educational research, with observations made in numerous countries around the world, the three most frequently observed types of teacher talk were as follows:

- *Rote*: the drilling of facts, ideas and routines through constant repetition;

- *Recitation*: The accumulation of knowledge and understanding through questions designed to test or stimulate recall of what has been previously encountered, or to cue students to work out the answer from clues provided in the question;

- *Instruction/exposition*: telling the student what to do, and/or imparting information, and/or explaining facts, principles or procedures.

(Alexander 2008, p. 110)

Less frequently observed, Alexander found that some teachers also used:

- *Discussion*: the exchange of ideas with a view to sharing information and solving problems;

- *Dialogue*: achieving common understanding through structured, cumulative questioning and discussion that guide and prompt, reduce choices, minimise risk and error, and expedite the 'handover' of concepts and principles.

(ibid.)

Later in his chapter, Alexander goes onto map certain types of teacher talk against the organisational interactions from the first repertoire. So, for example, we might suppose that if students are working within a collaborative group work context (i.e. without the teacher present), that teaching talk would contain more discussion and dialogue rather than rote or recitation. Some of you may recall the work of Vygotsky and his concept of the 'zone of proximal development'. Perhaps it is important to remember here that learning can take place 'under adult guidance or in collaboration with more capable peers' (Vygotsky 1978, p. 6). Done well, collaborative group work can result in powerful student-centred learning without you being involved!

That being said, the power of teacher talk is substantial. Before returning to Alexander's third repertoire, *learning talk*, it is worth considering in a little more detail how you can improve three of the key types of teacher talk that you will use to engage students in their learning:

1. Explanations.

2. Questioning.

3. Modelling.

1. Explaining things

Being able to explain something effectively is one of the most important skills that all teachers need. Almost every lesson that you teach will have a period of explanation within it at some point. Some people are born with an innate ability to explain things well. But for most of us, explaining things is a skill that can be learnt, practised and developed.

There are a number of characteristics or features of a successful explanation. In no particular order of priority, these include:

■ Using a hook of some sort to grab your students' attention and interest;

■ Having a key concept or idea that is at the heart of the explanation;

■ Varying your language, intonation and posture to emphasise specific points throughout your explanation;

■ Using signposting statements that signal a new direction within the explanation or help to summarise key points;

■ Using humour (which may or may not come naturally) to help a key idea remain with the student long after the explanation itself has finished;

■ Using examples from real life that help illustrate the key concept and establish students' understanding within a particular context;

■ Connect new ideas to students' previous experience or existing knowledge;

■ Utilise props or resources of various kinds to help add power and/or illustrate key ideas within the explanation.

An explanation is a vitally important part of most lessons. In the early days of teaching, you would be well advised to script your explanations, perhaps even writing them down word by word. Whilst we not advise you to read them out from a physical script, this mental preparation for this part of your lesson will be invaluable. Many of the points above (e.g. generating a hook for the explanation, incorporating contextual examples, signposting techniques, etc.) will all be difficult to do 'off the cuff' and need careful preparation. Explanations, like every aspect of your pedagogy, need careful thought and preparation in the vast majority of cases. Do not leave your explanations to chance. They will be ineffective and, at worse, will only serve to confuse your students.

So far, we have positioned the explanation as something that is under your control, delivered in a scripted way with little, if any, student involvement. This is only part of the story.

Explanations can be dynamic, entertaining, interactive and inclusive if you are able to think through how students will not only receive new knowledge or information, but how they will then go on to process that throughout the rest of your lesson. Much of this comes down to effective planning on your part. You will need to consider how your learning objectives for the lesson are not only explored within your explanation, but also developed through the teaching activities you have designed.

As with all of these three expositions on different types of teacher talk, explanations are mediated through your spoken language. Your ability to use language skilfully is essential. You will need to empathise with students, ask purposeful questions about the process of their learning (perhaps even within the explanation itself), consider the timing and pace of your delivery (are students able to keep up with you?), as well as the performance aspects of delivery (intonation, posture, etc.) that affect, at a fundamental level, how you communicate with your students.

REFLECTIVE TASK

Reflect back on an explanation that you have delivered to a class recently. Ask yourself the following questions:

- Were the key points of your explanation linked to the learning objectives of the lesson? Was this mentioned to the students?

- Where were the students sitting during your explanation? What were they doing? Were you able to actively engage them in any way during the explanation?

We'll return to the topic of explanations briefly in Chapter 7 and ask you to complete a more detailed task.

2. Questioning

Asking good questions is not just a matter of finding out what students know, but is also a way of developing learning and taking it forwards. Questioning is one of the most important student–teacher interactions, and accounts for a great deal of the talk that takes place in classrooms.

Knowing what sorts of questions to ask at what stage in the lesson is something that you will need to practise. Let us think about this by starting with the most obvious classification of question types; this is the difference between open questions and closed ones. Closed questions are ones that can be answered with single word or few words, and tend to be of the right/wrong variety:

- What's the capital of France?

- What's nine divided by three?

- Where is Brighton?

Some teachers decry closed questions, but for short and sharp checking of understanding they have their uses. Problems occur when teachers only ask closed questions. This is because for many closed questions you either know the answer, or you do not. There is very little chance of being able to work it out. For example, 'What is the key of Beethoven's sixth symphony?' If you know it is F major then you can answer, if you do not know, you can't go through a series of workings to arrive at the right answer. In class, when beginner teachers ask lots of closed questions, they are encouraged when they are answered. They may not realise that it is the same hands, and the same pupils who know. Pupils who do not know soon tire of this, and their attention wanders. This is a 'pub quiz' questioning technique. Another problem with this is that if you know that Paris in the capital of France, and get it right, you have not learned anything in the process. If you did not know, it is likely that the teacher has moved on to another question before you have had a chance to assimilate the information, and so the moment is lost.

Open questions require some working out of the answer, and in more than one word. Often open questions can also have more than one possible answer. 'Why is Paris the capital of France?' is a question that challenges, and will reveal information about the respondent. 'What is ten divided by five?' has one answer, 'Why does ten divided by five equal two?' requires the respondents to explain how they arrived at the answer that they provided.

Many teachers are familiar with Bloom's taxonomy (Bloom 1956), which is a way of classifying questions into a hierarchical form, starting with Knowledge (lower order thinking), and then moving towards higher order thinking (Analysis, Synthesis and Evaluation):

- Evaluation

- Synthesis

- Analysis   (Higher Order)

- Application

- Comprehension

- Knowledge   (Lower Order)

Notice that Knowledge, the lowest level of the taxonomy, is the one that features heavily in closed questions.

Using Bloom's taxonomy as a basis for questioning means that questioning is able to move from remembering to learning. Asking a question that requires higher order thinking makes the learners think about their answer, and weigh up a number of alternatives. To do this requires some practice to start with, and many teachers find it helpful to have a list of suitable question stems that they can use to formulate appropriate questions when the time occurs.

For beginning and student teachers, planning the questions you are going to ask in a lesson in advance may seem lengthy and tedious, but it is a good way of ensuring you do not get stuck in the closed/lower order rut!

Used well, questioning creates knowledge; used badly, prolonged pub-quiz questioning simply serves to emphasise differences between pupils, alienates those who do not know, and provides no new learning for those that do.

PRACTICAL TASK

Think about a lesson that you are going to deliver in the next few days. While you are planning the lesson, think about your strategy for using questions within the lesson. Ask yourself the following:

- What is a key question? (!)

- How many questions do I ask which are open/closed?

- How can I plan to ask more higher order thinking questions?

- What is higher order thinking in my subject?

- Can I ask a colleague to observe me and count the number and type of questions I ask?

3. Modelling

Modelling is linked to explanations, but for us it is a discrete skill with its own set of implications for the ways in which we might talk in the classroom. When we are learning a new skill or preparing to undertake a challenging task, it helps if we can:

■ See someone else do it first;

■ Hear them 'thinking aloud' about the decisions they are making;

■ Hear them explaining what they are doing at each stage;

■ Ask questions about the process as it is happening;

■ Identify problems as they arise and think aloud about how to solve them;

■ Slow the process down to look in detail at the most difficult part and ask for further clarification;

■ See the process demonstrated visually, sometimes repeated more than once if it is difficult to grasp;

■ Be given time to discuss what has been done and predict next steps.

(DfES 2004, p. 4)

This gives a good overview of what is involved when engaged in presenting a new idea, skill, concept, or technique to the class. It is especially important to notice the emphasis on slowing down and thinking out loud.

Thinking out loud is a key aspect of modelling, and it need not apply only to when doing something for the first time. It is a useful pedagogic skill to demonstrate the steps that you, the teacher, are undertaking when you work through to arrive at an answer. It is particularly useful when there is a series of stages that need to be gone through in order for the students to be able to do this by themselves. In many subjects the 'show your working' notion is an important one in written tasks; in modelling, the equivalent is thinking out loud. This requires a specific type of teacher talk that is different from that used within an explanation.

In psychology literature the idea of 'think out loud protocols' is well established. These are used when people are asked to talk through the thought processes they are engaged in when undertaking a task of some sort. This has a clear application in education, and it is useful for you, the teacher, to employ this technique whilst modelling a new skill or process in front of your students. Different subject areas will want to apply this in different ways.

Modelling can be applied more generically throughout teaching too; it need not just apply to subject specific areas. Many generic skills can also be modelled too. For instance, 'research skills', 'note-taking' and 'revision' are key components of many aspects of education. Modelling what constitutes good practice in these areas will require careful teacher talk to accompany the processes being illustrated.

PRACTICAL TASK

Identify a lesson in the near future when you are going to be introducing a new concept, skill or process to your students. Consider the bullet points above and plan a short modelling sequence for use within the lesson that utilises a 'think out aloud' portion of teacher talk. Script this carefully and consider the language choice and the mode of vocal delivery that you will adopt.

Following the lesson, reflect on the sequence of the lesson and, if possible, ask students whether or not they found it useful in helping them assimilate the new concept, skill or process you were seeking to teach them.

As we have seen, teacher talk in the classroom is an essential element for, an initiator of, your students' learning. Whether it be through your explanations, questioning, or the ways in which you model, there is plenty that you can practise here in terms of the words that you choose to use and the way in which you choose to deliver those words. More generally, it is interesting to reflect on the nature of teacher talk. The modern way is to encourage teachers not to talk too much. It is seen as a monological process and the antipathy of interaction and inclusion. However, nothing is further from the truth. Teacher talk can be captivating, engaging, inspirational and motivational done in the right way. Not many of us are born with these abilities, but it is worth pursuing them in a structured way and committing ourselves to getting better at these core communication skills.

Earlier in the chapter we were reflecting on Robin Alexander's three core pedagogical repertories. The first of these, the organisation of interaction, was touched on briefly and we have spent considerably longer considering the nature of teacher talk and the impact this has on student learning.

Alexander's third repertoire is *learning talk*. This is the talk of your students, and the 'forms of oral expression and interaction that they need to experience and eventually master' (Alexander 2008, p. 112). On the basis of research drawn from a significant number of countries across the world, Alexander notes that this includes students' ability to:

- Narrate;

- Explain;

- Instruct;

- Ask different kinds of questions;
- Receive, act and build upon answers;
- Analyse and solve problems;
- Speculate and imagine;
- Explore and evaluate ideas;
- Discuss;
- Argue, reason and justify;
- Negotiate;

together with four contingent abilities that are vital if children are to gain the full potential of talking with others:

- To listen;
- To be receptive to alternative viewpoints;
- To think about what they hear;
- To give others time to think.

(ibid.)

'Learning talk' is one of the key components of Alexander's framework for dialogic teaching that he incorporated within the most comprehensive independent enquiry into English primary education during 2006–2009 (a primary education review that was tragically and unforgivably ditched by the Conservative government when they came to power in 2010).

At the heart of dialogic teaching is a talk, a dialogue. It is beyond the scope of this book to develop this concept in too much detail, suffice to say that the role of the teacher in the dialogue is a crucial one with many dimensions.

In terms of teacher–student interactions, dialogic teaching requires teachers to think carefully about how they ask questions (in order to provoke thoughtful answers), sequence exchanges with individual students into coherent lines of enquiry rather than leaving students grappling with disconnected elements of conversations, and model good 'talk' which is clear, audible and expressive.

In terms of structuring student–student interactions within group work scenarios, it will be important for you to consider how you will encourage students to listen carefully to each other, how you can help them to encourage each other and build on each other's ideas, and respect minority viewpoints yet strive to reach a common understanding and agreed conclusions.

Here, for us and this chapter, one of the key messages is that you have a vital role in modelling these things for your students. As you learn to use your voice confidently and expressively, with a range of tone, pitch and intonation, choosing your words carefully for specific purposes and reasons, and adopting a broad range of expression, then your students will not only enjoy the process of being taught by you, but they will also learn vicariously to talk well throughout their lives.

Humour in the classroom

Before we close this chapter on your teacher talk and student learning, we wanted to explore one further important, if slightly more tangential, aspect of classroom interaction: humour. Our experiences of life generally prove that some people are just funnier than others. The same is probably true of our teachers. Will is definitely funnier than Jonathan.

As we write this section, we can recall those teachers who made us laugh regularly with a greater degree of detail and fondness, rather than the myriad of others who did not! This tells us something about the importance of humour in promoting students' learning.

The educational literature reinforces something that I suspect many of us know to be true from our own experiences of education already: the use of humour creates a positive atmosphere, reduces anxiety and facilitates the learning process (Berk 1996, 1998; Hill 1988).

So, can you learn to be funny in your teaching? To the extent that some people have a natural affinity towards humour as part of their individual personality, probably not. But all of us can learn to use humour in a constructive way within our teaching. According to Garner (2005), humour is most effective when it is appropriate to the audience, targeted within a specific topic, and placed in the context of the learning experience.

His article illustrates how humour can be linked to the use of metaphor and analogy in our teaching to help create positive associations in our students' minds that result in a greater chance of them remembering information, improve their critical thinking and create a positive and engaging classroom environment. It is available freely and well worth a read. This is something that we will explore further in Chapter 7.

Of course, everyone finds different things funny. One of the dangers of trying to be too humorous in the classroom is that you may alienate as many students (who do not find you funny) as those that you engage (and think you are the next great stand-up!). But, and perhaps you will not be surprised by this, educational researchers have even examined the appropriateness or inappropriateness of various types of humour in the classroom setting (Wanzer et al. 2006). This research identified four main types of appropriate humour:

1. Related humour: This included using media or other objects to enhance learning: jokes, stories, stereotypes, teacher performance, creative language usage.

2. Unrelated humour: Similar to the above but unrelated to the curriculum context being presented.

3. Self-disparaging humour: Making fun of yourself, telling embarrassing stories, etc.

4. Unintentional or unplanned humour: Unintentional puns or slips of the tongue.

In terms of inappropriate humour, the researchers document offensive humour, disparaging humour aimed at individual students related to their intelligence, race, gender or appearance, disparaging humour at 'other' targets as well as self-disparaging humour.

Whilst all this is probably extremely unfunny, it does illustrate the breadth of possible humour in the classroom. So, whilst our personalities are difficult to change (and there is a good argument in favour of not trying to be someone else whilst teaching!) it seems that it is possible to integrate humour of various types into our pedagogy. As with any new strand to your pedagogy, do not make drastic changes too quickly. Students see through thinly veiled and inauthentic pedagogical approaches very quickly. The best advice is probably to be yourself!

PRACTICAL TASK

Can you remember any good jokes? Why not look out some suitable content that is related to your subject and try a few out in a forthcoming lesson?

If you want something a bit more substantial to try out, metaphor and analogy are two related areas that fit well with humour in the classroom. Why not try bringing unusual ideas or concepts together in new ways and seeing how they spark off each other? Done well, this can take your talk and your students' learning into exciting, new and unexpected directions!

References

Alexander, R. (2008) *Essays on Pedagogy*. London: Routledge.

Bakhtin, M. M. (1981) 'The dialogic imagination'. (trans Emerson, C. & Holquist, M.). Austin: University of Texas Press.

Bakhtin, M. M. (1986) *Speech Genres and Other Late Essays*. Emerson, C. & Holmquist, M. (eds) (trans. McGee, V. W.). Austin: University of Texas Press.

Berk, R. (1996) 'Student ratings of ten strategies for using humor in college teaching'. *Journal on Excellence in College Teaching* 7:3, 71–92.

Berk, R. (1998) *Professors are from Mars, Students are from Snickers*. Madison, WI: Mendota Press.

Bloom, B. S. (1956) *Taxonomy of Educational Objectives, Handbook I: The cognitive domain*. New York: David McKay Co Inc.

DfES (2004) *Pedagogy and Practice: Teaching and learning in secondary schools* (Unit 6: Modelling). London: DfES (now DfE).

Garner, R. (2005) 'Humor, analogy, and metaphor: H.A.M. it up in teaching'. *Radical Pedagogy* 6:2. Also available from: http://radicalpedagogy.icaap.org/content/issue6_2/garner.html [last accessed 14/1/17].

Hill, D. (1988) *Humor in the Classroom: A handbook for teachers*. Springfield, Il: Charles C. Thomas.

Kroeker, K. (2004), 'Technology meets music: An interview with composer-singer Paul Korda'. *Tech News World*, http://www.technewsworld.com/story/32952.html [last accessed 23/3/09].

On Track and Field (2009) http://www.ontrackandfield.com/main/catalog/2009/polevaulthistory.html [last accessed 29/11/09].

Owen, M. (2006), 'The myth of the digital native'. http://www.futurelab.org.uk/viewpoint/art26.htm [last accessed 6/4/09].

Prensky, M. (2001) 'Digital natives, digital immigrants' *On the Horizon*, NCB University Press, 9:5, 1–6.

Rosenbaum, M. (2009) 'An illustrated history of pole vault'. http://trackandfield.about.com/od/polevault/ss/illuspolevault_2.htm [last accessed 30/11/09].

Salavuo, M. (2008) 'Are university students digital natives?' http://weblog.siba.fi/msalavuo/2008/09/12/are-university-students-digital-natives/ [last accessed 20/3/09].

Savage, J. (2007) 'Reconstructing music education through ICT'. *Research in Education* 78, 65–77.

Théberge, P. (1997) *Any Sound You Can Imagine: Making music/consuming technology*. London: Wesleyan University Press.

Vygotsky, L. S. (1978) *Mind in Society*. Cambridge, MA: Harvard University Press.

Wanzer, M., Frymier, A., Wojtaszczyk, A. & Smith, T. (2006) 'Appropriate and inappropriate uses of humor by teachers'. *Communication Education* 55:2, 178–196.

Wertsch, J. V. (1998) *Mind as Action*. Oxford: Oxford University Press.

Chapter 6

Developing an effective teacher voice

ICONIC VOICE PORTRAITS

Ella Fitzgerald (1917–1996) is a legend amongst jazz musicians. She is often referred to as the 'first lady of song' and the 'queen of jazz'. Her voice was known for its purity of tone, perfect intonation and its impeccable diction and phrasing. Ella also invented one of the most iconic forms of jazz improvisation with the voice: scat (improvised melodies using wordless sounds).

Her diction is excellent. Why? Look and listen into the support of very consistent air. This is coupled with excellent movement of the mouth to shape words. Her head is still, allowing support and shape of the words. She never makes an effort to be too loud or quiet, but there is a silky support of the air to give a big sound. The voice flows like a river of molten gold. Vibrato is used to colour the phrase.

Like most professionals, she makes it sound so easy. But the hours of practice that have gone into such good breathing, support and effortless shape are not easily spotted. It is far from effortless to develop such a voice, though.

Before becoming interested in singing in the early 1930s, Ella was a keen dancer and also attended church regularly with her parents. Here, she would have sung in the congregation, although there is no record of her taking part in any formal choral singing.

Having developed her singing informally and singing in an amateur capacity during the early 1930s, in 1935 she won the chance to perform for a week with the Tiny Bradshaw band at the Harlem Opera House. Through this work she met Chick Webb, a bandleader who was on the lookout for a new female singer. On meeting Ella, Webb wrote that he was 'reluctant to sign her . . . because she was gawky and unkempt, a diamond in the rough'. But, he did sign her and she became a regular in his band. The rest, as they say, is history.

This chapter will draw together the practical principles in the first five chapters. It will draw on the work of Matthew Syed who challenges theories associated with talent and practice. This chapter will dispel some popular myths about 'talent' and explain how practice is key in developing all one does as a teacher. It will consider how this practice can be built into your daily work so that it is an integrated part of all you do. Furthermore, it will briefly consider the inner challenges we all face as humans, teachers and professionals to have strong, confident and stress-free careers. In line with the key principles explored previously, we will help you build confidence in your vocal delivery as a core part of your personal and professional development.

In the first five chapters of the book we have dealt with some of the practicalities of how our human voices came about, why they are so important as a core part of our identity both as humans and teachers, and how the link between our ability to communicate and our lives together has evolved. We have considered how the basics of sound are produced and how you can apply these to the development of an effective classroom voice. In the previous chapter, we explored how your body language links to your vocal delivery to develop one integrated pedagogical approach.

After many years of working with teachers at all points in their careers, it is clear that there are many reasons why some teachers seem to 'naturally' develop a teacher's voice and others seem to struggle to understand or develop one. We will return to the idea of what is natural or not, soon, but perhaps it is better to draw together some key principles first so that we can consider them as a whole, begin to unpick their meaning and try to reconstruct them in a way that can help us consider this key point further.

To go back to where we started, consider why communication and language is so important in the world generally. What is it to communicate effectively and how is the simplicity and complexity of how we communicate so easily woven together? It is useful to also consider who you communicate with in your teaching and how important your audience, your students, are in effective communication. Consider why many elements of body language, room position and nonverbal communication, perhaps key to our ancestors' survival and competition, have now been subsumed in our modern, ultra-connected, society.

By now, hopefully, you are starting to consider the fundamentals or your voice, your sound and are doing this with increased understanding. By working through some of the tasks in the earlier chapters and by completing the exercises you are starting to better consider or understand what internal moving parts and actions control your voice. Better understanding of air, control, speed, pitch, timbre and articulation will be a lifelong learning experience. As we will consider further in Chapter 8, being engaged in this should not only serve to have a healthier longer career but also introduce new ways of communicating to yourself and thus new ways of working to your students. It will also start a cycle of understanding your voice and body so that you can better 'use it' to develop naturally. Vocal health, good posture and good sound can then support and benefit your teaching. Setting up processes that promote your general health and wellbeing in teaching is a very wise move! If you are starting out in teaching, it is a brilliant time to start as you mean to go on. If, like us, you are in the middle of your teaching career then it is never too late to make positive changes to your lifestyle and approach to teaching specifically.

The biggest factor we have encountered with all teachers who have struggled to develop their voice and communication is their strong conviction that having a 'good voice' is some sort of gift or given talent that you do or don't have. That you have a natural voice. The society that we live in seems to support this view in many respects. We use the terms 'gifted' and 'talented' without really thinking about what they mean or the trains of thought that might flow from them. From an early age children are surrounded with language that supports the idea that pupils are gifted, that others are somehow genetically superior to them, in certain tasks, thinking or skills.

REFLECTIVE TASK

What do you understand by the terms 'gifted' and 'talented'? What are the differences between the two terms? How have these two terms been used within schools over the last few years and what, in your opinion, have been the benefits or problems around their use?

There is much you can now read on coaching and development, especially in sport and music, that has gone to shift the paradigm on how we consider gifts or talents. Unfortunately, schools seem to support the idea that certain pupils are gifted or talented. The United Kingdom government published guidance in 2006 that was then updated in 2008 on 'identifying gifted and talented learners' (DCSF 2008). Clearly, different students will have different abilities. Some may show a particular aptitude for a certain subject and we would support the idea that good teachers know and understand the abilities of their students and how best to support their progress. The problem is labelling students by using standard sets of rules or criteria may skew your judgement about other students as well as perhaps limiting the choices for those students who have been identified as 'gifted' or 'talented' too. Systematising aptitude in this way can be unhelpful.

It is evident from Will's attending of a parents' evening just a few days ago that the words 'natural', 'talented' and 'gifted' are overused and often ill-considered. Having seen our children develop, we can understand why some of these words might be used in common parlance. But what are we really describing here? Is being gifted just being better at something, at a skill, than others of a similar age? How would that work in comparing children at different ages? Would we still describe a young footballer as gifted at five years old if they were compared to another one at 16 years old? Is it about potential? Or, is being gifted being able to seemingly advance or improve at skills more quickly than others of a similar age? As teachers, would we seek to understand this in a broader contextual way? Do we consider the practice or rehearsal that goes on at home and the associated level of parental support or resource that underpins that child's progress? Is being gifted linked to how much a student enjoys something? If they enjoy art, it is likely that they will do more of it in their own time without seeing it as a task or a chore. Is this taken into account when we seek to identify the 'gifts' or 'talents' that our students have?

In our first teaching jobs, we encountered several teachers who said that they could spot or identify very quickly pupils who were gifted and talented in their subjects. Will even encountered a violin teacher who refused to teach certain pupils after an initial ten-minute lesson if they couldn't do certain musical tasks. This teacher believed that if you didn't have certain listening skills it was pointless wasting his or the students' time in beginning violin lessons as at some point they would all realise that there was no point and no progress as they didn't have the basic 'listening gift'!

We would suggest that there are many problems in seeing our students or ourselves as limited in this way. Think about the example of the violin teacher. Is it really possible to identify musical talent on the basis of some quick musical tests done in a sterile context where the student doesn't know or understand the particular agenda of the teacher, where they are likely to feel stressed, anxious and nervous whilst probably wanting to make a good impression? Is this a fair way to seek to understand a child's musical potential? Limiting the opportunities that students have based on their current skill levels seems like the wrong approach. But how often do we apply this lesson in our own lives? How much of this 'talent spotting' takes into account the journey that the student has already taken?

Schools are certainly good in dealing in absolutes. Students understand from a very early age that there are correct and incorrect answers. Clearly, on one hand this is a good thing, but on the other hand it does result in you often focussing on what you can't do rather than what you can do. When learning is done to a set criteria of success rather than as a way to develop and nurture skills we already have, it may limit how we perceive our own skills or abilities. Jonathan was delighted when one of his young children came home from primary school with a new 'golden rule'. His young daughter told him that her teacher had said that no one was allowed to say 'I can't' anymore. Instead, they have been told to say, 'I'll try!' We need more of this positive attitude in our schools today.

So, what are the steps to developing a great teacher voice?

Step one: You have unlimited potential

So, step one to developing an effective teaching voice is to realise that you aren't limited in your vocal capacities. You are just a product of your experiences so far (good and bad). Other teachers whom you meet who have a more 'natural' voice are just a product of a different set of experiences so far. These will be linked to their physical development, their encounters throughout their life and associated experiences. You are different. You can develop from where you are. The key is being able to understand where you are on your journey and, from there, to plan your own developmental learning journey.

We feel that many of the 'natural' skills that people have are often driven by a media obsession to create celebrity in sportsmen, musicians or actors. As we are both long-standing fans of Manchester United, we have long wondered whether Wayne Rooney really does have a football brain, or whether David Beckham became good at free-kicks just because he had few friends to actually play football with? Or, thinking about some of the iconic voice portraits that we have included at the beginning of each chapter, whether some famous singers like Ella Fitzgerald would be seen as gifted if they had worked within a different style or genre of music. Like all things, natural talent cannot be seen outside of the context within which it is developed.

As musicians we have long been interested in this and we have had several case study conversations with highly rated musicians and young sports players. Glenn Van Looy is a well-respected, young, virtuoso euphonium player. At the age of 26 he had accomplished many things that other musicians would never be able to achieve. So, is Glenn a gifted player? Has someone given him his gifts? Well, in conversation it is clear that it is no accident that Glenn is 'gifted'. His father was also a brass musician, a bass trombonist and he encouraged Glenn to play at a young age. He quickly 'fell in love' with the euphonium and played in the local wind band that his father conducted. He was soon to advance into more prestigious bands and ensembles at an early age, fuelling his love for his instrument and practice. In Glenn's words though, there was little else to do in the little village where he lived so playing his instrument was fun, time consuming, and soon to become an enjoyable obsession.

Peter Moore, the fabulous trombonist, has had a similar meteoric rise to fame. At 12 years old, he won the BBC Young Musician of the Year and has gone on to set records that will struggle to be matched, including becoming the youngest ever principal trombonist in a professional orchestra. Was Peter gifted? Did he find his skills or was he given them by someone or something? Again, his story is similar to Glenn's. His father was a player, conductor and music teacher. Peter was most likely introduced to playing at an early stage with a good focus of support and practice. Peter in his words didn't formally practise much (as Will heard him say in a master class) and, as Sloboda notes, this is quite common amongst successful professionals: 'many subjects seemed to find it difficult to recall with any certainty whether they had done more or less informal practice than formal practice' (Sloboda 1991, p. 301).

When speaking to his father some years before though, he told Will how Peter was 'obsessed with his trombone' and would pick it up as soon as he could after getting back from whatever he had been doing. He told me how they would have to take the instrument off him to get him to do other things or go to bed. But I suppose that Peter loved this. He didn't see it as a task to practise, he enjoyed it so much that to him it was as 'natural' as the hours that some children will spend on computer games, watching YouTube videos or interacting through social media.

There are also many examples you can read in sport. But what seems to support all of these stories of 'gifts or talents' are that they were nurtured in some way at an earlier age to start *purposeful practice*.

> An investigation of British musicians ... found that the top performers had learned no faster than those who reached lower levels of attainment: hour for hour, the various groups has improved at almost identical rates. The difference was that top performers had practiced *for more hours.*
>
> (Syed 2010, p. 13)

Step two: Practice and purposeful practice

Step two in developing an effective voice is to learn how you practise purposefully. This is not just repeating what you are already doing. You need to enjoy the practice process and spend many hours doing it in order to improve. But what is 'purposeful practice' as opposed to just 'practice'? Colvin explores this by considering how he has learnt to play golf. Some readers will recognise this experience:

> We all know what practice is. I do it all the time. Odds are good that you do it in a similar general way, regardless of what you're practicing. When I practice golf, I go to the driving range and get two big buckets of balls. I pick my spot, put down my bag of clubs, and tip over one of the buckets. I read somewhere that you should warm up with short irons, so I take out an 8- or 9-iron and start hitting. I also read somewhere that you should always have a target, so I pick one of the fake 'greens' out on the range and aim for it, though I'm not really sure how far away it is. As I work through the short irons, middle irons, long irons, and driver, I hit quite a few bad shots. My usual reaction is to hit another ball as quickly as possible in hopes that it will be a decent shot, and then I can forget about the bad one.
>
> (Colvin 2008, p. 65)

Ericsson describes purposeful practice as 'deliberate practice':

> In contrast to play, deliberate practice is a highly structured activity, the explicit goal of which is to improve performance. Specific tasks are invented to overcome weakness, and performance is carefully monitored to provide cues for ways to

improve further. We claim that deliberate practice requires effort and is not inherently enjoyable. Individuals are motivated to practice because practice improves performance.

(Ericsson et al. 1993, p. 10)

But couldn't this deliberate practice still be seen as play? If you really enjoy what you are doing, do you see the hard work that might be involved in it? Deliberate or purposeful practice seems to be somewhere between just enjoying what you are doing and really focussing and working on it.

The idea of purposeful practice is also discussed in Syed (2010) and Sloboda (1991 & 1994). Is purposeful practice what separates those seen as 'gifted' or 'talented' from everyone else? Did Glenn and Peter do 'purposeful practice' from an early age?

Purposeful practice is clearly a complex thing but it can be broken down into several layers. Colvin suggests that it contains the following:

- It's designed specifically to improve performance;

- It can be repeated a lot;

- Feedback on results is continuously available;

- It's highly demanding mentally;

- It isn't much fun.

(Colvin 2008, pp. 67–71)

Let's take each of these key points in turn and consider them a bit further.

1. Designing a programme of development

To really practise you have to work out a way of specifically trying to improve your voice. You will need to consider your motivation for wanting to improve and what support you might need. Ask colleagues to observe you, read lots, collect video and audio data and reflect on this. Then try things that specifically focus on improving a specific element of your voice. Focus on individual elements such as pace, air, pitch, body position, etc. to gain specific insights through purposeful practice routines.

PRACTICAL TASK

Through video, audio or feedback from a colleague choose a focus for your voice development. From our experience it can be best to work on air and breathing first. Try to practise what different air speeds and amounts of air feel like.

Practise some breathing exercises to support this. Practise a short amount of shouting to consider what the air speed feels like. Practise a quite big voice. This needs good support of a large amount of air but for the air to leave the body as slowly as you can.

You could just as easily work on pitch. Discuss with a colleague using evidence the pitch of the voice you most often use. Try varying this. Try practising using several different pitches during lessons. Give a focus of real practice to this.

2. Repeated practice

You need then to repeat this. You need to give the practice time and you need to critically evaluate its progress. Again, use support to collect data and reflect in this. One of the good things about teaching is that there is a fair amount of opportunity for repeated practice. But don't confuse routine with purposeful practice. You must keep your developmental aims at the forefront of your mind.

PRACTICAL TASK

Make a logical timetable of when and where you are practising your vocal work. Link this to point 1 here. You don't need a class to practise, but you do need to put time aside to practise regularly. Like most things, ten minutes a day is better than five hours on one day each week. You also need to plan a warm-up and warm-down period to go with this practice.

3. Feedback

The loop of purposeful practice has to be supported with continuous feedback. Working with others can really help here. Clearly, your access to other members of staff's time will be limited. But, you have a captive audience who can be involved in helping you improve. Why not include your students in this journey? Many will be receptive to your desires to improve your teaching and will offer you interesting insights into what you are doing. This can be done explicitly or implicitly. In other words, you might tell certain students that you are trying to work on a specific aspect of your teaching and you'd welcome their feedback; or, you just become highly observant to their behaviour and conversations within the classroom and try to ascertain what impact your vocal delivery is having on their learning.

Feedback also separates the idea of just doing something for enjoyment and really focussing on something to improve. We really hope that you enjoy the whole process of teaching. It is a demanding job that clearly most folk don't do for the money alone! Committing yourself to a purposeful practice routine is a sign of your passion to be the best that you can be as a teacher.

That said, it is important that you don't lose the playfulness that is essential to being a good teacher. Psychologists write about this in respect of 'formal' and 'informal' practice activities. Here's Sloboda writing about each and their benefits for musicians:

> There are grounds for predicting some relationship between informal musical activity and achievement. It has been suggested (Sloboda, 1991, 1994) that playful exploratory musical activities are likely to encourage the development of expressivity in performance, whereas formal practice is likely to be more directly influential with respect to the development of technique.
>
> (Sloboda et al. 1996, p. 289)

PRACTICAL TASK

Plan how you can collect regular feedback to give you time to reflect critically on this data. Video or audio recorders over time will give an excellent support of progress you make. This will also support you at moments when you might want to falter from the efforts this takes.

We understand the stresses and strains of teaching each day so acknowledge that knowing this is work will help you keep going.

4. Hard work

Purposeful practice is hard work. It will be mentally and physically demanding. Done well, you will make progress but you will also make mistakes. The 'mistakes' are part of the learning so use them in a productive way to help improve your vocal delivery further.

5. By doing this we might remove the fun

Focussing so heavily on ourselves to perform, collect data and practise in a meaningful way will not always be fun. Like many people who are training to teach would verify, it isn't always easy to change and develop personally (and teaching is a very personal and demanding thing). It may not feel like fun but, as these routines, skills and abilities develop, it should return to being a natural part of what we do. Doing something well will eventually become fun.

If it seems a bit depressing that the most important thing you can do to improve performance is not always fun, take consolation in this:

> It must be so. If the activities that lead to greatness were easy and fun, then everyone would do them and they would not distinguish the best from the rest. The reality that deliberate practice is hard can even be seen as good news. It means that most people won't do it. So your willingness to do it will distinguish you all the more.
>
> (Colvin 2008, p. 72)

Step three: Practice doesn't make perfect

In order to develop a great teaching voice, you will need to practise purposefully. There are no shortcuts here. However, it is important to realise that even purposeful practice won't result in a perfect teaching voice. Let's start with another sporting example.

Jonny Wilkinson, the ex-England rugby union player, is England's highest points scorer. Many of his points were achieved by kicking the rugby ball between the rugby posts (a conversion). As anyone who has seen Jonny play will know, he did this in a very particular and precise way:

> He clearly has a very set routine of how he practices and executes his kicks. In his own words 'When the whistle blows for a penalty, I'm immediately thinking – where are the posts? What's the wind like? How will I line this up?'
>
> (BBC 2009)

He then takes a tee (a rubber mould within which the rugby ball sits) and lines the ball up in a very set routine. There is then a measured set of steps back, then to the side; he then part crouches and brings his hands together, much like praying. In these final seconds he can take in wind direction, distance and aim before kicking. Very little of what he does can be about kicking the ball. So why do it?

Jonny Wilkinson here is portraying a very set practised routine. A routine of purposeful practice. This will do two main things. Firstly, it helps him to focus and complete this task under extreme pressure on the sports field. It elevates worry in the task. He follows the same routine he has practised hundreds of times so there is less room for error.

Second though, because the routine is so purposeful or deliberate it allows him to obtain a new set of experiences in relation to that kick. From his perspective, hopefully it will result in a successful outcome (and more often than not it did). But even Jonny is not perfect. If an element did go wrong, if he missed the rugby posts, he was still able to more readily focus on the difference or change that caused the error thereby helping to eliminate this for the next opportunity that came along.

So, purposeful practice has more than one end to it. It is important to develop your own routines related to elements of your voice, body and communication to get the most from the time and effort you put in. But be aware, there is no quick fix, it takes time. Sloboda again:

> [the data involved in the paper] have fully confirmed the existence of a strong positive relationship between practice and achievement. . . high achievers practice the most, moderate achievers practice a moderate amount, and low achievers practice hardly at all.
>
> (Sloboda, et al 1996, p. 306)

The point of deliberate practice is not to make something perfect but to develop more effective routines so that you continually improve. The teachers who are most successful are those that see their work as continual development, as having no set end point other than to keep enjoying what they do and improving.

Importantly, developing routines will build better work into your practice. Deliberate work will not always be so effortful.

Think of this in how you have learned any skill. Driving, teaching, sport or musical? There are so many that you could think of in your own life.

Consider how much you had to think about this as a novice teacher. Curran's work on the brain (Curran 2008) shows us that when you are starting out with a new activity you are principally using the frontal cortex of your brain. You are having to think a lot about what you are doing. Have you learnt to drive? To start with there is so much to do! Check around yourself, over your shoulder, gear, clutch, brake, handbrake, accelerator, indicators . . . how could you ever be expected to do all of this and stay alive? But, over time, routines kick in and you are able to think about other things (watching the road, avoiding pedestrians and other important components of driving safely!).

The same experience is replicated when you start teaching. You have to remember a lot: the lesson plan, all the activities, the register, all the things your mentor has told you, talking, organising, setting tasks, collecting in homework, evaluating everything that moves, whilst, all at the same time, trying to communicate with 30 adorable children and trying to come out the other side of the lesson in one piece!

As we become more proficient in these activities, we programme our malleable brains to do this far more naturally. As we practise, purposefully, we wire our brain and the neurons within it into pathways or networks that allow us to do these things more 'naturally', more 'skilfully' (more like a gifted individual perhaps). This is why someone who is good at something looks like they are doing it easily; they are. They have stopped considering it all and are using the more internal limbic brain to support these professional skills.

You, too, can develop this in your voice and body language by focussing and developing purposeful routines over time. But don't be too hard on yourself. Practice doesn't always make perfect, but purposeful practice will help you improve.

The term 'shed's gone' may not mean much to many of you reading this. The term is often used in musical circles to describe a moment when someone is overcome by nerves. The normal result is in failure to play a part well. Many people may have experienced a moment of anxiety or panic when having to do something under pressure. When it all goes wrong, then 'shed's gone'!

One of the most famous sporting moments of this might have been the golfer Rory McIlroy's 'melt-down' at the 2011 US Masters. He entered the last round of play with a four shot lead but lost this. What was surprising was not losing such a major event but the manner in which it happened. For whatever reason on that day, something caused Rory to forget his routines and overthink what he was doing. We could argue that he moved from the deep limbic centres of the brain where he had practised to become an expert. He brought his frontal cortex to the fore (no pun intended), and was thinking in the moment. In many ways, for a brief period in that final round he returned to being a beginner with devastating effect.

Of course, we now know that he would recover from this experience and go on to achieve great things in the sport, including winning major titles and becoming the world's number one player. He is a good example of how we can learn from a moment of nervous failure.

To develop an effective voice, you must first consider why you want to? You then need to plan to evaluate where you are now, what are your strengths and weaknesses. You need to plan to develop, not change, the individual parts of your voice. Over time, you need to develop a routine of purposeful practice so that you can make improve yourself and become a professional at this. Remember, so far, we have found no evidence of gifted individuals or natural teachers! If you're good at something, you've practised for a long time and in a purposeful way!

Start your purposeful routine with the tasks in this chapter. In summary:

1. Pick a point to focus on.

2. Plan and practise this.

3. Collect data, get feedback and reflect on this to develop the routine, not the skill.

4. Keep developing new routines of purposeful practice to develop new elements, combining over time new ways of working.

Remember not to focus on what you perceive as a problem or on 'getting louder' or just talking more slowly. Work on the basic elements of the voice and body to develop your whole voice. Develop practice to improve your basics of breathing, production and delivery.

References

BBC (2009) http://news.bbc.co.uk/sport1/hi/rugby_union/get_involved/4204746.stm [last accessed 31/4/17]

Colvin, G. (2008) *Talent is Overrated: What really separates world-class performers from everybody else.* London: Penguin Books.

Curran, A. (2008) *The Little Book of Big Stuff about the Brain*. Carmarthen: Crown House Publishing Ltd.

DCSF (2008) 'Identifying Gifted and Talented Learners – Getting Started'. http://webarchive.nationalarchives.gov.uk/20130401151715/http://www.education.gov.uk/publications/eorderingdownload/getting%20startedwr.pdf

Ericsson, K. A., Krampe, R. & Tesch-Romer, C. (1993) 'The role of deliberate practice in the acquisition of expert performance'. *Psychological Review* 100:3, 363–406.

Sloboda, J. A. (1991) 'Musical expertise'. In Ericsson, K. A. & Smith, J. (eds) *Toward a General Theory of Expertise: Prospects and limits*. Cambridge: Cambridge University Press.

Sloboda, J. A. (1994) *Musical Perceptions*. New York: Oxford University Press.

Sloboda, J. A., Davidson, J. W., Howe, M. J. A. & Moore, D. G. (1996) 'The role of practice in the development of performing musicians'. *British Journal of Psychology* 87, 287–309.

Syed, M (2010) *Bounce: The myth of talent and the power of practice.* London: Harper Collins.

Chapter 7

Metaphors for teaching and vocal performance

ICONIC VOICE PORTRAITS

There will be very few of us that can't recall the sound of Martin Luther King's 'I have a dream' speech. Out of all the speeches given by humans over the centuries, perhaps this one is one of the most famous not just because of the nature of King's vocal delivery but also because of the way in which the key ideas within it were structured and developed through various techniques that King had honed throughout his life and experience in church and in politics.

Reflecting on the speech, Catherine Carr (Carr 2017) has identified a number of other related points about the speech and why it has become such a seminal moment in American history.

First, it was delivered at an iconic location, on the steps of the Lincoln Memorial. It touched the heart and the head, through using references from the Gettysburg Address as well as the Emancipation Proclamation, the Constitution, and Declaration of Independence. But academic weight was balanced with stirring rhetoric of the heart, quoting passages from scripture and also a Negro spiritual.

Throughout the speech, King used vivid language and metaphors to help reinforce key points. For example, in this passage he used the metaphor of the cheque to highlight the lack of justice that black Americans had experienced:

> In a sense we've come to our nation's capital to cash a check. When the architects of our republic wrote the magnificent words of the Constitution and the Declaration of Independence, they were signing a promissory note to which every American was to fall heir. Instead of honoring this sacred obligation, America has given the Negro people a bad check, a check which has come back marked "insufficient funds." But we refuse to believe that the bank of justice is bankrupt. We refuse to believe that there are

insufficient funds in the great vaults of opportunity of this nation. And so, we've come to cash this check, a check that will give us upon demand the riches of freedom and the security of justice.

Another key feature of the speech is King's use of repetition to make his message stick in the audience's minds:

Now is the time to make real the promises of democracy. Now is the time to rise from the dark and desolate valley of segregation to the sunlit path of racial justice. Now is the time to lift our nation from the quicksands of racial injustice to the solid rock of brotherhood. Now is the time to make justice a reality for all of God's children.

This is a technique that we have seen used on many occasions by America's first black President – Barack Obama.

King's message was also clear and compelling, ending on a note of hope, of aspiration. As Carr writes, few of us will ever reach the dizzy heights of Martin Luther King's words or acquire his competence in our vocal delivery. But it certainly gives us something to consider and to aim for.

Teaching involves a huge array of activities. Many of these take place in private but, as we have discussed throughout the book, the 'performance' of teaching is very public and builds on a range of skills that you will need to master, including good vocal presence and delivery. To illustrate this further, lesson planning is normally a solitary, private activity that invokes many skills, including (but not limited to):

■ Diagnosing and setting appropriate learning objectives;

■ Choosing relevant and purposeful teaching activities;

■ Designing assessment and differentiation frameworks;

■ Assembling or producing helpful resources;

■ And much more besides!

This private process comes to life within the classroom. But just consider for a moment how the actual planning you have done on paper (or on screen) impacts on the actual delivery of the lesson within the classroom. Does it? We would argue that if the lesson planning has been done well it should have a significant impact on how you speak, move and act within the classroom. Whilst not many of your students will ever ask to see your lesson plan, you will be the live 'version' of that lesson plan and present it to your students through your whole 'performance' of that lesson. Your pedagogy is the vehicle by which this embodiment and transformation can take place.

This 'embodiment' of the curriculum in your pedagogy is worth pausing to consider in a little more detail. What is it that you are 'embodying'? It will include the general way that you speak and act. These will include models of behaviour, communication and collaboration that you demonstrate in your dealings with students, other staff, parents, the caretaker and cleaners, and others; it will also include your seriousness in promoting active engagement in teaching and learning within your classroom. Second, in a more specific way, whether you are teaching in a primary or secondary school, you are the vital first point of contact in relation to the specific subjects that you teach your pupils. For secondary school teachers, the science curriculum documentation may be in place but you, as a teacher of science, represent that subject – day in, day out – for your students. Like it or not, you 'live' science for them by the way that you speak, act and behave as a teacher and scientist in your classroom. This has significant consequences for the way that you will teach science.

The same is true for primary school teachers. As you will have to teach a broader range of subjects and topics than your secondary colleagues, you need to be a passionate advocate for all the subjects that you teach, whether or not you feel that you are a specialist in that particular area. You will need to draw connections between them and show your students how an active and positive engagement with a broad range of knowledge, skills and understanding can result in a happy and fulfilled life. In this sense, students really do take the lead from you. If you want them to be enthusiastic, be enthusiastic yourself; if you want them to be engaged and motivated to learn, then you have to lead by example and provide that earnest and serious approach to support their learning that they deserve.

Your own professional development and the curriculum development go hand in hand. They work together in an intimate way. Think about this in relation to the lesson planning you are doing. How do you feel about the lesson plan that you are putting together? Does it capture your imagination? Does it excite and inspire you as a teacher? Can you visualise yourself giving an inspiring performance in the lesson? If it does not, can you really expect it to inspire your students? Are you finding it hard to make natural links between the various sections of the lesson? Do you know what you are going to say at key moments and how you are going to say it? Is the narrative of the lesson clearly identifiable? Have you built in signposting sections for the students to take notice of? Does the lesson have a clear beginning, middle and end? If the answer to any of these questions is no, then it is probably unrealistic to expect the majority of your students to engage with and make sense of your lesson either.

Most dictionaries define pedagogy as 'the science of teaching'. Like any metaphor, there are going to be benefits as well as limitations of such a conception. On the plus side, science implies a clear process of enquiry. Doing 'good' science relies on defining key principles, utilising appropriate methods, carefully handling materials, being precise and rigorous. All these things could be considered as being part of a good pedagogical approach too. Additionally, planning is a central component of 'doing' good science. Do you remember practical science lessons where experiments were modelled by the teacher at the front of the classroom before you did them on benches around the laboratory? A key element of this approach is the experiment 'method', which has to be written up clearly and concisely as part of an account of the experiment. Last week, I had to go to my son's Year 8 parents' evening. He likes science and I spoke with his science teacher who was generally complimentary about his work. Unfortunately, for him, the one downside of his work was that he rushed the writing up stage of the work. To be honest, I remember doing the same (but please don't tell him that!). In science, it is not enough to merely find out the correct answer to a particular scientific problem. The process by which you have come to find out that answer has to be represented and accounted for in order for others to replicate that experiment and test your findings. Being able to write this process down in clear steps was an important part of 'doing' science well. This rule applies for Year 8 boys in exactly the same way as it would apply to someone wanting to publish a scientific study in an academic journal.

But as with any metaphors there are limits to the idea of teaching being a science. As we explored through this book, it is often not possible to find the perfect mix of pedagogical ingredients and then mix them together in the desired quantities, according to a particular method, and – hey presto – you become a perfect teacher! Teaching is built on human relationships and these do not lend themselves to be easily reducible to basic component parts. That said though, there is merit in the rigorous exploration of the specific elements or characteristics of a pedagogical approach, including how you speak and what you say within the classroom. Finding ways of accounting for this in the 'method' of pedagogical enquiry would be a useful exercise at this early stage of your career. It might involve you doing a detailed and focussed observation of a particular element of your pedagogy.

PRACTICAL TASK

In Chapter 4 we focussed on how you can develop your body language alongside your vocal communication. Ask a colleague to make a video of you teaching and then analyse your own performance using the following starter questions:

- Where do you stand/sit throughout a lesson? (Plot your movement through a diagrammatic chart the represents your movement throughout the lesson.)

- What posture do you adopt (describe it in detail) and how does this flow from one posture to another?

How do you use your hands to emphasise key points (when does this happen and how does it relate to the language you are using and the tone of your voice)?

What barriers are there which inhibit your body language and can these be removed?

Or, in Chapter 5, we considered in detail a number of specific types of teacher talk including explanations, questions and modelling. In the following practical task, use your phone to record yourself delivering an explanation during one of your lessons.

REFLECTIVE TASK

Listen back to the audio recording and reflect on the following questions:

How is the explanation structured (does it have one)?

How does it relate to the key learning objectives that have been established within the lesson?

What hooks are used to engage the pupils' curiosity (and are these an aide memoire for students later on)?

How are key points repeated or re-emphasised throughout the explanation?

What, if any, scaffolding devices are used? Are references made to existing knowledge structures and, if so, how are these extended?

What, if any, links are there to modelling and how does this relate to any explanations that are given?

How are the learning outcomes for the lesson highlighted or hinted at through the explanation and/or model?

This kind of detailed, almost forensic, analysis of a specific pedagogical technique or device can produce very rich learning experiences for you. However, as we emphasised above, just conducting the observation and finding out the 'correct' answer to your enquiry, will not automatically translate into your being able to adopt an appropriate body language in the classroom, or explain new concepts better. Defining pedagogy as 'science of teaching' has its limitations.

So, alongside this first metaphor of 'teaching as science', we can bring a range of other metaphors into this debate. In Chapter 3 we considered one of these when we considered how teaching could be related to acting. Here, we will look at another one of the performing arts – music. Like teaching, the work that musicians do in a performance builds on a specific set of skills and techniques, various pieces of knowledge and a broad understanding of the music they are working within. It also relies on them giving brilliant performances using their voices or instruments! Like teaching, these skilful players also engage in planning and preparation (they might call it 'rehearsal') that is often done in private and normally prior to a performance.

Teaching as musicianship

Performing musicians in many traditions are often required to work with a score that has been produced by a composer. This can take many different forms but perhaps the most common would use a range of specific music notation including clefs, notes and other performance instructions. The score is the basis for a performance, however it does not contain everything that is needed in order to give a convincing performance. As we saw with the actor's script in Chapter 3, the musician's score has to be interpreted in light of a number of factors.

These factors are informed by the musician's understanding of the specific performance conventions that surround the period of time when the music was written or the style that it exhibits. So, for example, a musical score from the Baroque period of music (e.g. the work of Vivaldi) would need to be approached in a different way to a score produced by a Romantic composer such as Brahms. Part of this is because of the amount of detail that such a score may or may not contain. There is a general movement in the history of music for scores to contain more and more detail within them as they get closer to the present day. For example, Vivaldi might have been quite happy to tell his musicians to play quietly or loudly; Brahms' scores contain very precise instructions about the volume of specific passages of music within his score, as well as the gradual changes of volume that might occur over a period of time. The same is true of many other aspects of music's composition and performance. By the twentieth century, the musical score itself had become a very detailed representation of the composer's wishes that the performing musician had to take notice of and reproduce faithfully. For some, the musical score itself had become an object to be valued above anything else. By the end of the twentieth century, many composers had sought to replace the musician themselves and communicate with their audience directly through tape, and later, digital recordings of their music which, to a larger extent, were under their own control through specially prepared recordings or other mechanical reproductive technologies.

The element of control that a composer can exert on a musical performer through a musical score is only part of the story, though. All composers expect musicians to play within a particular style that is suitable for their music. Vivaldi would have expected his musicians to provide embellishments to his score (perhaps by adding particular musical effects at key moments to enhance the beauty of a particular melody); Brahms would have frowned on his musicians playing his music in this way and conductors of his music today would also not allow musicians to improvise. By contrast, in many operatic styles the Da Capo aria became the vehicle by which singers were able to show off their vocal virtuosity. Here, the basic structure of the aria (song) contained two main sections – part one and part two. Following the performance of part one and part two, the first part would be repeated but it would be quite wrong for the singer to perform it in the same way as earlier in the aria. The singer was expected to take the basic ideas of the song (the melody) and transform it through their virtuosity into something significantly different. In other words, they had to reinterpret the emotions and feelings within part one in light of the ideas contained within part two. As opera shifted from a private to a public form of entertainment in the early nineteenth century, audiences would pay vast sums of money to hear specific singers (virtuosi) interpret these Da Capo arias in this way. This resulted in many composers, and others, complaining that the overall narrative of the opera was being hi-jacked (or at least put on one side for the duration of the aria) by the singer for their own personal fame and notoriety.

As with the actor and the world of the theatre, there are some interesting comparisons here to the work of teachers in planning and delivering a lesson. Firstly, as with the previous example, teachers are in that dual position of composing the lesson plan (the score) and delivering it (through their performance); they have a joint role of composer and musician. Our exploration of the role of the score in musical performance raises questions about the amount of detail that may or may not be necessary in the lesson plan and the extent to which any individual teacher needs to be held accountable to the lesson plan as an integral part of their performance.

As a young teacher, you may decide to include a lot of information in your early lesson plans. This may help you feel confident during the lesson and give you a series of signals or signposts to help you along the way. You may feel the need to script key sequences of text in relation to an explanation or a series of questions that you will want to deliver. You may want to write down reminders to yourself about particular modes or styles of delivery and use contrasting colours to help these instructions to yourself stand out in the hurly burly of the lesson. But, over time, you may be able to manage with less detail, perhaps just writing down the general structure within the plan itself and allowing space for its embellishment through your pedagogical performance.

The metaphor also allows us to explore an interesting element of audience (student) expectation here. To what extent should the lesson plan and the activities therein build on the 'legitimate' sense of student expectation within lessons? Like the singer performing a Da Capo aria, the endless repeating of familiar ideas needs to be avoided.

The skilful embellishments and extemporisations that a teacher can bring to existing subject content is something that can provide endless challenge for all of us. No two performances of a Da Capo aria should be the same; similarly, no two lessons taught to any group of students, will ever be same (even if they have the same or very similar lesson plans underpinning them). Should you use the same lesson plan for similar lessons? Our answer is always no! Whilst certain elements may be similar, the group of students you are teaching in any one given lesson are a unique group. They should not be treated the same.

Additionally, the stylistic differences between different types of music have some relevance here too. There are differences in subject approaches to lesson planning and delivery that you will need to bear in mind. For those of you training to be primary school teachers, you may find these differences overwhelming on occasions. This is because they reflect more than just technical differences, but go right to the heart of what individual subjects really are and what they try to achieve as part of a student's formal education. Lesson planning should not look or feel the same for every subject.

For those of you working in the secondary school context, it is important to look beyond your subject boundaries regularly. You will find that there are significant benefits to your own pedagogy as a geography teacher if you go and spend some time looking at how the drama teacher encourages his students to find their individual voices; as a music teacher you will find significant benefits in looking at how the science teacher organises and curates the various resources needed for a complex experiment. This kind of pedagogical cross-curricularity is something that I have noticed on many occasions when we have visited schools around the North West of England. Perhaps the most interesting example that relates most closely to our discussion of the work of actors and musicians is drawn from the work of one drama teacher I saw teaching a Year 8 class (Savage 2012). In the lesson I saw the teacher made an explicit link to a pedagogical device drawn from the world of the theatre, her 'home' subject. This device was then applied for a new purpose within the classroom. Whilst this might not be considered 'cross-curricular' in the traditional sense, it does reveal an approach to teaching a subject that builds upon its wider heritage and the tools or processes within it.

The specific technique used throughout a significant portion of the lesson was called 'freeze framing'. During the lesson, and as part of a unit of work on developing a character's identity, students were improvising a scene that depicted Rosa Parks' refusal to give up her seat on a bus for a white passenger in Montgomery, Alabama. At key moments, the teacher would shout 'Freeze!' and the students were required to stop what they were doing and remain absolutely still and quiet. At this key moment, they are asked to reflect, in character, about their feelings at that specific moment. In the drama teacher's words:

> I find it a very helpful way to try to understand whether or not the pupil really understands the role of their character. I make use of a technique called 'freeze

framing'. This is when the action in a particular scene of frozen at a particular point in time. Normally I will decide when this happens, although sometimes I will let pupils decide. At the particular moment when I shout 'Freeze!', every pupil involved in the scene has to stop what they are doing or saying and remain absolutely still. They stop moving, talking or anything else. This allows us to think together about the situation that the pupils are presenting through their acting. It is a technique drawn from the theatre and it allows a particular actor to talk about their perceptions in the situation they find themselves in or to give the audience further information about how they might be feeling or thinking. Some directors called this 'thought tracking'.

(ibid.)

In an interview, I asked the teacher why she had adopted this tool. Again, in her words:

As a teacher, I use this technique quite a lot to help my understanding of whether pupils are really engaging with a particular scene. I would say it is a key part of my assessment for learning strategy. During the freeze frame moment I will ask questions to a particular character in the scene. Sometimes I will also ask pupils who are watching the scene with me to ask questions too. I find it a very helpful way to try to understand whether or not the pupil is really understands the role of their character. Obviously it has limitations. In drama, pupils often feel things that they can't express in words. But, when used with other assessment devices, freeze framing is a really useful assessment tool. And I'm pleased that it is an adaptation of a tool from the theatre.

(ibid.)

REFLECTIVE TASK

For those of us who are not drama teachers, we could ask ourselves an obvious question: what would 'freeze-framing' look like in our subject area?

For all of us: what are the key pedagogical techniques in our own subject areas and how could these be shared with other teachers?

Teaching as coaching

We hear a lot about coaching in education at the moment. In most sports at least, the role of the coach is distinct from that of the teacher. For a moment, let's consider the work of footballers and how a metaphorical reflection on them can help us consider our pedagogy in a new way. We have chosen to focus on their work for a number of reasons. Firstly, there are a number of similarities with the work of actors and musicians

– they work in a group, they are highly skilful as individuals, and they provide a 'performance' (of varying quality perhaps depending on your opinion of your team!). But in contrast to the vast majority of actors and musicians, footballers do not have a script or a score to work towards. Or do they?

During the early summer of 2012 there was a significant change in the management of the England football team. It caused a lot of press speculation. Whilst the press and many pundits initially favoured the appointment of Harry Redknapp to the position, the appointment of Roy Hodgson in May 2012 came as a surprise to some. One of the concerns that was raised at the time related to the coaching style that Hodgson was purported to favour (Zonal Marking 2012). Whilst working at various clubs around Europe, some professional footballers had found his coaching style too heavy-handed and laborious, involving them walking through particular team movements in what was seen as a stifling way. Pundits jumped on this observation and contrasted it with the work of other football managers who, it was claimed, allowed their players a platform to exhibit their own flair and creativity. In summary, Harry Redknapp, some claimed, was 'all about individuals'; Hodgson, in contrast, was 'the ultimate system manager' (ibid.).

The consequences of these approaches to coaching and team management can be seen by any keen football supporter. Sitting towards the back of a football ground, it is possible to observe the 'shape' of the football team ebbing and flowing as they move between defensive and attacking positions. The 11 players, whilst each being highly skilful and tactically aware as an individual, should be playing as part of a larger team that has to be flexible enough to accommodate and rebut the advances of the other team whilst maximising their own potential to attack and score when the right moment arises.

A metaphorical reflection on the style of coaching that footballers receive gets to the heart of the relationship between lesson planning and lesson delivery. Taken to an extreme, the 'certain anarchy' (ibid.) style of management represented by the work of Redknapp and others could result in a pedagogical style that is all about a teacher's individual flair, exhibitionism and personal charisma. To these teachers, perhaps, the requirement for careful, systematic planning for learning that covers all eventualities (akin to the system management approach of Hodgson) is an anathema. They need to thrive on the freedom and flexibility of their individual talents and not feel encumbered by pedagogical rules or regulations. But for others, a planning approach that covers every square inch of the field, and every eventuality, is seen as preferable. Within that clear structure, these coaches would argue, the individual flair of specific players can be nurtured and developed. For teachers following this model, very detailed planning might be seen as a requirement for teaching that will facilitate every student's learning to their full potential.

But unlike actors and musicians, the footballer metaphor has one unique element that has a massive impact – another team to compete against! The opposition are coached and drilled to exploit your own team and your individual players' weaknesses, and are there to beat you within the rules of the game. Here, we are not conceptualising your students as the opposing team! Rather, we would like to suggest that they do provide the challenge to any teacher's planning and pedagogy. Your challenge is to match your own personal strengths, flair to the development of a pedagogy that captures and inspires their imagination, making them enthusiastic about their learning and keen to participate fully in your classes. They will also provide that 'grit' against which your teaching will be honed.

In our job we are often asked what makes the perfect teaching placement. Some students imagine that the independent schools, with their small classes and beautifully behaved children would be perfect for them! Well, first of all, we are not sure that this is always the case. But, more importantly, very well behaved, passive classes are often the hardest to teach well. A lively group of pupils who respond to your lesson (in good or bad ways) will often give you that immediate feedback that you need as a young teacher to change tack, provide additional support or add more challenge. The perfect teaching placement is one where students are challenging but where you have good mentor support to be able to cope with that challenge and, over time, develop your own individual pedagogy to meet those challenges on your own.

Planning, pedagogy and vocal delivery

Metaphorical application and reflection can really help us think differently about the processes of teaching, the development of an effective pedagogy and how your voice and vocal delivery can be enhanced in your teaching. These performance metaphors raise a number of key points.

First, all performance activities do require preparation and planning of some sort. In acting (Chapter 3), music and football (discussed above), being well prepared with technical skills, stylistic awareness, communication skills and a good sense of team-work are all necessary criteria for success. These things do not happen by accident. They require dedication over many years, regular practice, analysis and a constant focus on reflection and evaluation of one's own practice. Whilst actors and musicians often work with a script or score, and this imposes certain restrictions on them, even footballers are working within a particular 'system' that may constrain the opportunities for any one player's individual action. In all cases, having a framework for artistic or sporting action is essential to the success of the activity. For us as teachers, the dedication that we need to work on our own pedagogical approach must be undertaken with the same degree of seriousness and long-term commitment. As we have said throughout our book, the development of your voice is a long-term project that you need to commit to. The consequences of not doing so, as we will see in our final chapter, can be dire. (Prepare yourself for some challenging lessons from the research into teachers' problems with vocal health.)

Second, in all these metaphors there is a tension between the script, the score or the coaching strategy, which all seek to impose on the work of the performer, and the desire of the creative actor, musician or footballer who wants to bring their own sense of personality and vision to their work. This could be interpreted as a desire to conform or liberate. Perhaps the moments that an audience most value are when an actor, musician or footballer is able to take that step out of conformity and bring something that is unique and of the moment to that particular audience? However, that process of liberation can be taken too far. We would not want our Shakespearian actors to deviate from the script into some kind of free-flowing narrative; nor would we expect a right-back with defensive duties to abandon his team mates and adopt a careless forward role within a football game. For young teachers, sticking with your lesson plan is a vital first step towards creating this link between planning and pedagogy. You have to lay the groundwork for a more liberated approach to teaching in the conformity of the lesson plan. There is no short cut. Whatever the strengths of your own individual teaching ability, they will need to be honed and developed through the three-staged process of planning, teaching and reflection.

Thirdly, even with the most highly improvisatory forms of theatre, music and team management, there are mental frameworks and schemata within which performers work. This is important. Musical improvisation, when musicians apparently make music up on the spot (combining composition and performance together in the moment) is, essentially, an illusion. Improvisatory musicians have a framework of musical ideas in their minds, generated through hours of practice and pre-rehearsal; improvising jazz musicians have highly developed stylistic languages to draw on, developed through their listening to recordings, so playing one type of chord for Ella Fitzgerald might be highly appropriate whilst for Billie Holliday it would transgress her style.

For teachers, apparently making up lessons on the spot should be avoided but experienced teachers will often talk about their best lessons coming to them in an instance, perhaps whilst doing something else completely different. These moments do not appear out of nothing. There will have been a systematic exploration of that particular field of subject teaching and pedagogy that underpins that creative moment. Creativity in lesson planning can happen, but it happens against the backdrop of hard work and effort (in our experience, 99% perspiration and 1% inspiration).

Applying metaphors in your own teaching

This chapter has taken a playful approach to the use of the metaphors to help explore your voice, your identity and your pedagogy. We have utilised a range of approaches here, many of which have a very useful application to teaching more generally. Using metaphors in this way can help provide us with alternative insights into routine activities. As a slight aside to the main topic of this book, we thought that we would take a model for the development of productive metaphors drawn from the work of Eikenberry (Eikenberry 2009) and adopted by the NASAGA (NASAGA 2009). The 3C Model provides a helpful structure for applying metaphors to learning contexts. It is based on two premises. Firstly, that the brain works by building connections and associations between concepts and ideas; secondly, that the brain remembers more easily things that are unusual or novel. The three-stage model incorporates the following three steps: Create, Connect and Combine. This model will be introduced in a practical task that will help you apply metaphors to the teaching of a lesson that introduces a new concept to your students. We hope that you will find it useful.

PRACTICAL TASK

1. Create

Determine which lesson you want to focus on. Make sure you allow yourself plenty of time to complete this element of the planning process.

A. Write down all the key elements of the topic that you want to cover during the lesson. This would include trying to sketch out some key learning objectives and outcomes for the lesson.

B. How do you want to teach this? Think about the type of teaching or learning activities that you might want to incorporate within the lesson. It would also include examples you might use in the explanatory parts of the lesson. Write down any ideas you have in simple, non-jargon/technical language. This will help you see potential metaphors more easily. You can afford to be quite experimental here. Do not rule out ideas at this stage.

C. At this point you are going to begin to compile a list of metaphors for use within the lesson. Go through the list of key elements that you have constructed. What do these remind you of? Use free association techniques to help here. How did you remember these elements when you were learning about them? This is a creative process and some of the ideas may be odd, strange or incomplete. This does not matter at the moment. Write them down anyway.

D. Do a random association exercise. This would include:

  – Creating a random list of words (there are loads on the Internet) or choose one of the productive metaphors identified in (c);
  – Select a word from the list;

- Is the word you have chosen like one of the key elements that you want to teach? Perhaps it is not? One word may not give you an immediate connection. But it may lead you to another word that does spark an idea.
- Capture your ideas by making short notes. The random words you are using may become the metaphor you ultimately want to use in your lesson;
- Repeat this process by picking another word from the random word list.

E. From all your notes to this point, pick one or more of the really promising ideas. Perhaps you have identified different possible metaphors for different pieces of lesson content, or perhaps you have an overall metaphor for the lesson. The key point here is to try and make a provisional decision about what you want to implement within the lesson. Make sure you are enthusiastic about it! If not, repeat the process but choose a different key element (back to part 1b).

You are now ready to move onto the next stage.

2. Connect

In this state you are going to make connections between the key elements of the lesson and the metaphor(s) that you are going to adopt within the lesson.

Compare the metaphor idea with the lesson content. Write down the potential metaphor and some general elements of that idea. Compare these with the ideas about the lesson content. Ask yourself the following questions:

- How are the general elements of each connected?

- How are they alike? Are there any key differences?

- Can you use phrases from the metaphor to describe steps of parts of your content?

- Are there key differences that you will need to be aware of, and possibly make learners aware of?

- Are there any potential confusing elements related to the metaphor, or the way that you have applied it, that will stifle the instructional use of the metaphor in your lesson?

3. Combine

The final important step determines how you are going to combine or integrate the metaphor within the flow of the lesson. This will have implications for your use of language, the design of any teaching resources to accompany your lesson and, perhaps, any accompanying assessment framework or processes. The following questions and answers from the NASAGA materials (NASAGA 2009) may help you build on your ideas. But, as they point out, they are only suggestions and you may find yourself diving off into completely different directions. Just remain focussed on the learner experience in the lesson and try to plan for the best possible approach to teaching in this cross-curricular way with metaphors as you can.

a. Can I introduce the metaphor before the lesson, perhaps in a previous lesson or in a previous homework task?

Maybe your metaphor will become a theme for the lesson. In preparation, pupils could be encouraged to bring something, wear something, be thinking of something related to the metaphor in advance of the lesson. This may raise your pupils' level of anticipation for the lesson and have beneficial results.

b. How will I introduce the metaphor to the group?

In this example, perhaps you have chosen a metaphor for a specific purpose during the lesson rather than as a general theme (as in the above example). In this case, you might want to use the metaphor in the explanatory part of the lesson. If you can help pupils construct a mental framework for the metaphor then this will help them piece together new content against this framework at a later part of the lesson. Of course, visual or kinaesthetic frameworks are excellent at doing this. Try and make use of these, including any interactive (physical or virtual) elements that you can prepare, as often as possible.

c. What could I do visually to enhance the connection between my content and the metaphor?

As mentioned in the previous answer, there are many options here. Using the wall space in the classroom can help (see Savage 1999 for one example of how this was done to good effect). Put up graphics or pictures of the metaphor or its component parts. Use a theme on any presentational and class materials that you prepare for the lesson to accentuate the metaphor.

d. What other senses can I use to solidify the metaphor?

Think about other senses beyond sight. How can pupils engage their sense of touch (perhaps through a model or toy), smell (actual or related), or hearing (sound effects, other noises)? I remember watching a lesson about musical form, which included binary, ternary and rondo forms (basically an AB, ABA and ABACA structure respectively). The trainee teacher brought this to life by making a basic hamburger in front of the class. Binary (AB) became the bottom half of the bun and the burger; ternary (ABA) placed the top of the bun on the top part of the burger; rondo form involved placing another burger and top part of the bun on top of the existing 'ternary' burger (it ended up looking like a Big Mac)! I was not sure what it tasted like, but it smelt good and I am certain the pupils remembered their musical forms for a while.

e. How can I reinforce the metaphor in the conclusion of the lesson?

Make sure that you reinforce the metaphor through repetition at the end of the lesson, by referencing it in your plenary and using it to help structure questions that relate to the new content taught alongside the metaphor. Ask students to summarise the new content, using the metaphor and any associated frameworks as a guide.

This chapter has taken key themes from earlier in our book and reconsidered them through various metaphors. In the final chapter, we will be considering some bad news! Poor vocal health amongst teachers is a real danger. The research evidence is overwhelming. Brace yourself, but also remember that there will be good news in the chapter too. The solutions to ensuring that you have a strong, healthy voice that can sustain a long and enjoyable teaching career are in your hands.

References

Carr, C. (2017) 'What made "I have a dream" such a perfect speech?' https://www.fastcompany.com/3040976/what-made-i-have-a-dream-such-a-perfect-speech [last accessed 1/4/17].

Eikenberry, K. (2009) 'The Kevin Eikenberry Group'. http://kevineikenberry.com/ [last accessed 5/1/10].

North American Simulation and Gaming Association (NASAGA) (2009) 'Creating metaphors and analogies to use in training and other learning events'. www.nasaga.org [last accessed 15/12/09].

Savage, J. (1999) 'Approaches to composition with music technology'. http://www.jsavage.org.uk/jsorg/wp-content/uploads/2011/03/Approaches-to-composition.pdf [last accessed 31/03/17].

Savage, J. (2012) 'Moving beyond subject boundaries: Four case studies of cross-curricular pedagogy in secondary schools'. *International Journal of Educational Research* 55, 79–88.

Zonal Marking (2012) 'England appoint Roy Hodgson'. http://www.zonalmarking.net/2012/05/01/england-appoint-roy-hodgson/ [last accessed 3/11/12].

Chapter 8

Looking after your voice

ICONIC VOICE PORTRAITS

Terry Wogan was a much loved Irish radio and television broadcaster who, for the majority of his career, worked for the BBC. Perhaps he is most famous for his Radio 2 breakfast show, which was regularly listened to by over 8 million people each day, and his witty commentaries to the Eurovision Song Contest were often the only reason we tuned in watch!

Behind Wogan's relaxed style, there was considerable vocal skill and dexterity. Wogan used his voice and his words to create an atmosphere in which you felt he was chatting directly to you, the listener, using humour alongside sympathy and empathy at times, to make you feel as though you were sharing your morning cup of tea with him. This has led many to think that Terry was simply the greatest light broadcaster of all time.

Wogan's Irish accent is as gentle as it is distinct. It has a relaxed delivery, an unthreatening manner with a good degree of self-deprecation. He had an ability to gently muse on things out aloud and, at times, present ideas in a teasing manner. This, combined with his good humour, was the genius of his style of delivery.

Writing about Wogan's impact of broadcasting, and considering him alongside other broadcasters like Ken Bruce and Sarah Kennedy with regional dialects, Matthew Paris wrote this in *The Spectator:*

Subliminally, most British listeners react badly to upper-class male voices unless they are royal, like Prince Charles, or eccentric, like Brian Sewell. . . . You see their secret, don't you? We English, the vast majority of their radio audience, are unable to place their accents in class terms. There are, of course, upper and lower class accents in Ireland and Scotland, but the English do not know how to read them and distinguish. With the

> possible exception of a thick Glaswegian accent or deep Irish brogue, Scots and Irish accents are classless to English ears. This enables us men (sic) to relax and stop feeling threatened. The same is true of the male American, Canadian and Australian voices we warm to on the BBC. The conclusion is clear. If you want to get on in British broadcasting, son, choose Dublin or Edinburgh for your university education, and try to pick up the accent.
>
> (Paris 2007)

Welcome to the final chapter of our book! Well done for making it this far. We hope you have found it useful and that the lessons contained herein have proved useful for your teaching practice.

We've saved some worrying news for the final pages of our book. For us, at the midpoint in our careers, it addresses one of the key issues that we have noted in our friends and colleagues who have enjoyed 20 or so years of teaching. Looking after one's voice is a key part of all vocal development and it is essential if you are to enjoy a long and productive teaching career. Sadly, too many teachers soon find that their voice is strained, damaged and a worn-out tool. In this chapter we will consider how you can complete the daily act of teaching and communicating with large groups of students without damaging your voice as an instrument. We will also unpick bad habits so that you can re-learn better methods and ways of working.

It is estimated that between 5–10 per cent of the workforce are 'heavy occupational voice users' (Titze, Lemke & Montequin 1997). This group includes a very wide range of occupations, including those working in telesales, members of the clergy, tour guides, actors, singers and lawyers. However, it is teachers who represent the largest group of professionals who use their voice as a primary tool of their trade.

Despite their prevalence within this group, the number of substantial studies about teachers and their propensity for voice disorders is remarkably few. In one of the largest studies done within the states of Iowa and Utah (comprising 1,243 teachers and 1,288 non-teachers), researchers found that the reporting of a voice problem was significantly higher in the teachers' group compared with the non-teachers' group (11 per cent compared with 6 per cent). Furthermore, the prevalence of voice disorders over the course of a lifetime was even greater, with 58 per cent of teachers having a problem at some stage in their career compared with 29 per cent of the non-teachers (Roy et al. 2004, p. 281).

What is meant by the term 'voice disorder'? This varies in the literature, but for Roy et al. (ibid.) a voice disorder was considered to be 'anytime your voice does not work, perform, or sound as you feel it normally should, so that it interferes with communication' (ibid., p. 283). Their study showed that of the 1,088 teachers who reported experiencing a voice disorder during their lifetime:

- 19 per cent had a chronic voice disorder (i.e. lasting four weeks or more);

- 81 per cent had an acute voice disorder (i.e. lasting less than four weeks);

- They were more likely to report multiple voice disorders episodes;

- They were more likely to have visited a physician or speech–language pathologist about their disorder;

- The prevalence of voice disorders increased with age, peaking in the age group of 50–59 years;

- Women had a higher prevalence of voice disorders compared with men (46 per cent compared with 37 per cent); and

- Women also had a higher prevalence of chronic voice disorders compared with men (21 per cent compared to 13 per cent).

(ibid., pp. 284–285)

However, the research also revealed that non-teachers were more likely than teachers to report chronic problems (17 per cent versus 22 per cent). They say:

> This finding indicates that teachers may be prone to frequent, but short-lived, voice problems (i.e., less than 4 weeks in duration) and is generally consistent with the report of Marks (1985), who indicated that only 10% of teachers surveyed reported voice problems that lasted more than 6 days. It may be that teachers experience some degree of tissue repair over weekends, holidays, and vacations when occupation-related voice demands are lessened and vocal fold tissue injury is reduced.

(ibid., p. 290)

REFLECTIVE TASK

Whatever stage you are at in your teaching career, have you noticed that your voice has been strained or damaged at any point? Can you pinpoint a particular moment when this happened or did the strain creep up on you unannounced? How long did the vocal disorder last for? Did you have to get any medical help or were you able to rest your voice to allow it to recuperate naturally?

Your voice and its physical environment

Whilst the majority of this book has focussed on you as an individual and the development of your own teaching voice, it is important to remember that this voice will both develop, and be used every day, within a particular physical space – your classroom. Research into what is known as 'voice ergonomics' has identified a range of risk factors that can impact on the development of an effective teaching voice (Rantala et al. 2013). Voice ergonomics is part of a strand of work that falls under the remit of health and safety protocols and legislation designed to protect you from ill-health. There is also the obvious benefit that a better speaking environment will also improve the ability of students to listen because it increases speech intelligibility.

So, what are key risk factors that might impact on the development or production of a good teaching voice in your classroom? The research would suggest that there are four main areas:

1. Your working culture. As we have seen from our discussions earlier in the book, the working culture of schools and teachers can be the cause of significant risks to your vocal development. The research shows that teachers talk longer (Masuda et al. 1993), louder and at a higher pitch than most other working professionals (Hunter & Titze 2010; Titze et al. 2007). The consequent 'vocal loading' (i.e. the strain that is placed upon your voice and its speech organs through this sustained use), feeds into this negative spiral of a culture where voices are raised and strained in an unhelpful way (Laukkanen & Kankare 2006; Laukkanen et al. 2008).

2. Your posture. As we have explored through the second half of Chapter 4, poor postural alignment impairs your voice production. It also increases with the incidence of voice symptoms. Common problems include what speech pathologists and physiotherapists call 'forward head thrust' (Kooijman et al. 2005). This is often linked to other problems of postural alignment, which can also have detrimental effects on vocal production. A thorough exploration of these can be found in Arboleda and Frederick (2006), which contains a description of the three most common postural misalignments together with a range of exercises to help form the basis of a clinical intervention to help form a normal postural alignment. The misalignment of the head is particularly important for your vocal production. A misalignment here will impair voice resonance (Wilson Arboleda & Frederick 2008), the production of lower pitches (an important element of a resonant voice, see 11), and a tensing of the external laryngeal muscles with long-term negative consequences (Rubin et al. 2007).

3. Air quality. This is an interesting one! Researchers have found that factors including unpleasant odours, dryness, dustiness and temperature can all have negative effects on vocal production. There are numerous examples that could be cited. Poor indoor

air quality correlates with increased voice symptoms and laryngitis (Rantala et al. 2013; Kooijman et al. 2005); damp or mouldy air exacerbates asthma symptoms and other allergies with the consequent negative impacts for voice symptoms (Mendell et al. 2011; Simberg et al. 2009); when the air is too dry the viscosity and stiffness of laryngeal mucosa increases (not a pleasant topic, we appreciate), and the voice range profile narrows (Witt et al. 2011; Sihvo 1997); dust triggers allergic and inflammatory reactions in the larynx and laryngeal mucosa too (Sala et al. 1996).

4. Noise. This is the most common and most highly reported risk factor to your voice production. Exposure to excess noise, even noise that is defined as low intensity, is associated with increased sickness absence (Clausen et al. 2013), as well as the potential to interrupt ongoing activities and disturb the perception of speech (Shield & Dockrell 2003, 2004). In a national survey of Danish teachers, researchers reported that 59 per cent of teachers were exposed to a high level of noise that 'disturbed their work activities' for a least 1/4 of their working time (against an occupational average of 42 per cent) (Kristiansen 2010).

If the risk factors associated with a good and healthy voice are clear, the significant risks associated with the activity of teaching and the development of vocal problems are also very clear in the research literature, too. In one of the largest literature reviews into voice disorders in recent years, Cutiva, Vogel and Burdorf (2013) analysed the findings of 214 academic papers from three major health databases and found the following startling statistics:

■ Teachers had a significantly increased occurrence of voice disorders compared with other occupations;

■ Several work-related factors were consistently associated with voice disorders, including high levels of noise in classrooms, and poor physical environments with their associated poor acoustics;

■ Teachers working with larger class sizes were three times more likely to report voice disorders than teachers working with smaller classes;

■ Teachers of physical education and performing arts were more likely to report voice disorders than those of other subject areas;

■ The younger the pupils the more often voice disorders will be prevalent. The vocal load exhibited by teachers of primary and pre-school pupils was higher than that reported by teachers within secondary schools;

■ There is a substantial amount of evidence that points to a gender difference here, with female teachers reporting more vocal disorders than male teachers;

▓ The link between voice disorders and the length of time teaching is unclear. There is some evidence that older teachers exhibit more signs of vocal disorder, but there are other studies that show the opposite effect. Researchers urge caution here (Cutiva et al. 2013, pp. 149–150).

In summary, the research literature shows that the majority of teachers will suffer from some kind of vocal disorder during their teaching careers. Teaching, by its nature it seems, results in more disorders than almost any other occupation. These disorders are as a result of having to speak with increased effort for long periods of time. Teachers will not have long periods of rest during an average working day or week; this can only exacerbate the problem. Other factors include age, gender, a lack of technological resources (e.g. amplification systems to help teachers reinforce their voices, of which more below), buildings with poor acoustics, excess noise and poor posture. The impact of these vocal disorders on teachers is substantial. Teachers are more likely to become stressed and anxious, days will be lost through sickness absence and some teachers are forced to take early retirement.

PRACTICAL TASK

Spend some time thinking about the physical environment that you teach in. How would you describe it? Out of the list of things that have been discussed in the first part of this chapter, are there specific things that you recognise in your workplace?

What, if anything, can be done to ameliorate these? Are you aware of the health and safety legislation that is in place to protect you as a worker within your workplace? If not, ask to look at the school's health and safety policy and find out what it says in relation to the physical environment. You are entitled to work within a safe environment. If these environmental factors are not addressed appropriately then you have clear grounds to make formal complaints to your employer to address these.

More positively, although the problems associated with voice disorders are becoming well known and explored within the research literature, the potential prevention strategies and treatments are also clearly identified and are frequently low cost and relatively easy to implement. In their study, Szymanowski, Borst and Sataloff (2014) report that a three-pronged approach proved particularly effective.

Firstly, teachers undertaking a short course in vocal hygiene and prevention were compared with a control group of teachers who received no instruction. Three months hence, the study group's voices were analysed against a voice handicap index, mean phonation time, and other measures. Their voices showed significant improvements in vocal load, roughness, breathiness, asthenia and strain compared with the control group. Twelve months later, the same teachers were examined and although the improvements were not as pronounced they were still evidenced in the data collected.

Meta-analysis of 74 articles associated with voice disorders amongst teachers conducted by Awan (2013), identified that both indirect and direct forms of voice therapy are beneficial for teachers. 'Indirect' forms of therapy included making teachers aware of issues associated with vocal health and hygiene (including the avoidance of behaviours that can have a detrimental effect on the vocal fold, e.g. excessive throat clearing), improvements in hydration. Direct forms were reported as having more significant benefits. These included training teachers in direct vocal training, voice characteristics and vocal efficiency. In their conclusions, they write that

> ... both individual and group vocal health interventions may produce some benefits for some teachers with voice problems. While vocal health intervention produces better results than no intervention at all for teachers with voice problems, the benefits from vocal health interventions appear poorer than benefits from actual direct voice training programs (with or without vocal health instructions). Vocal amplification to help reduce vocal loudness during teaching has been reported to provide favorable results and may provide improved clarity and ease of voice production vs. direct voice therapies.
>
> (Awan 2013, pp. 58–59)

In other words, prevention is better than cure! Learning about your voice and how to look after it, and training yourself in how to use if efficiently in the classroom, is the best way to avoid vocal health issues later in your teaching career.

Second, as noted in the above quote, the use of voice amplification in the classroom can be particularly beneficial for those teachers that have already developed a vocal dysfunction. The improvements were considerable, and compared very favourably to those achievable through the vocal hygiene and prevention training route. Clearly, there is a cost associated to such provision but this needs to be weighed against the potential other negative effects of not addressing the problem. We will be turning our attention to possible technological solutions that you could use in your classroom in the final pages of this chapter.

Third, various voice training methods have been shown to have varying degrees of benefit for teachers. The efficacy of resonant voice therapy is noted as being particularly effective with vocal fold pathology, vibration patterns and voice quality all improving after as little as eight weekly sessions. This type of training also compares favourably against the more limited respiratory muscle training when compared using various vocal health assessment matrices.

Whilst the prevention strategies and treatments vary from place to place, and whilst researchers will argue about their efficiency and associated cost benefit analyses, the important point to remember here is that your vocal production can be improved. Yes, teaching is a risky activity for your vocal health. But being aware, taking precautions, and learning to use your voice productively and safely are key steps to ensuring that you don't damage your voice and, better still, learn to use it confidently and creatively as an essential part of your teaching presence.

The acoustic environment

Your voice is not something that exists in a vacuum! If it did, no one would be able to hear it (and you probably wouldn't be able to hear it or use it either – but our knowledge of the precise science behind this is pretty limited!).

You use your voice in physical spaces that may, or may not, have been designed with any consideration given to the acoustical properties required for an effective teaching and learning space. Many school buildings are very old and will, by nature of their age, not reflect the principles associated with good acoustic design; even newer buildings can be put together quickly and not really facilitate the activities that will go on within them (we know this as music teachers whose very subject is noisy! Perhaps we should take this opportunity to apologise to all those teachers who have had to teach their subjects next to music rooms with the associated spillage of sounds like African drums, glockenspiels and keyboards!).

Studies exploring aspects of 'acoustic comfort' within schools identify a number of features that impact on classroom acoustics (Puglisi et al. 2015, pp. 3097–3098):

- *Sound insulation*: This includes measuring the noise difference between various different materials (such as plasterboard, concrete, carpet, etc.) in terms of reflection and absorption. Key measurements would be taken at various points within a school building, including in-between adjacent classrooms (whether next door to each other on the same floor or above/below each other on different floors), and between classrooms and corridors;

- *Reverberation times*: This refers to the decay of sounds in the classroom space. These will vary at different points within the classroom. The times will also vary dramatically depending on whether the room is full of people or not;

- *Clarity*: Researchers can measure 'clarity' using various indices related to scales of 'speech transmission', 'voice support' and 'room gain'. This gets a little too technical for our discussion here but the key point is that everything located within the classroom space impacts on the clarity of the sound and its reception at any given point;

- *Background noise*: Whilst physical materials, bodies, design and other factors will influence acoustic comfort in a classroom, the background noises associated with spaces external to the classroom itself will impact on acoustic comfort. In a modern school building that we visited recently, the central heating ducts and trunking acted as a vehicle for the transmission of sounds from other rooms above or below the classroom where we were observing a lesson. This was a rather peculiar sensation (imagine ghostly voices and other background sounds) and one that we found disconcerting. The teacher and students in the room had just got used to it!

PRACTICAL TASK

If you are in the fortunate position of being able to spend most of your time teaching in one classroom, spend some time thinking about the acoustics of the space. Whilst restructuring the space itself is probably going to be impossible, what can you do with the things in the space itself to break up straight lines of reflective surfaces to mitigate the effect of sound waves bouncing around uncontrollably? Soft furnishings can really help with this (e.g. curtains, drapes, absorbing materials on sofas, cushions). You don't necessarily need to spend a fortune on expensive sound absorption tiles to make a huge difference in the acoustics of a room. It will make your and your students' lives much more enjoyable too!

Classroom noise

By its very nature, teaching can be a noisy activity. Whilst some subjects are noisier than others (and we both taught one of the noisiest – music!), contending with class-room noise is something that all teachers have to learn to manage. However, noise is something that can be studied in a range of occupations and it is interesting to read about how noise can impact on you as a professional and compare that to other professions too.

A recent Danish study has investigated the extent to which school teachers are exposed to noise in the course of their work. They studied whether noise posed a risk to teachers' hearing and also analysed the association between classroom acoustical conditions, noise exposure, vocal symptoms and cognitive fatigue (Kristiansen et al. 2014).

The study reported that the average noise level during the lessons that the researchers observed was around 72 dB. This increased slightly (around 6 dB) for certain types of activities such as indoor sports. They reported that the room reverberation times, which were measured as being between 0.39 and 0.83 seconds, did not have a significant effect on the noise level.

However, the study found that teachers were talking with a raised voice 61 per cent of the time and that their vocal load increased by 0.65 dB per 1 dB increase in the average lesson noise level. An increase in voice symptoms correlated significantly with the increase in noise exposure. This also resulted in a decrease in teacher performance. The researchers also found that there were no risks associated with noise-induced hearing impairments as a result of undertaking work as a teacher. But, the results did provide evidence for an association between noise exposure and vocal load and the development of vocal symptoms and cognitive fatigue once the teaching episodes had concluded (ibid., p. 858).

These findings have been replicated in a further study by Rantala et al. (2015) in which 40 teachers from 14 primary schools were randomly selected for the study. Ambient noise was measured during break-times throughout the day and compared against the noise caused by students' activities within lessons. The researchers recorded vocal samples from the teachers throughout the day and compared them in terms of their sound pressure level, their fundamental frequencies and other technical elements.

In most situations, the source of classroom noise is the sound of children undertaking classroom activities. In that sense, noise is a desirable thing because it probably means that your students are undertaking the activities that you have asked them to undertake in an active and participatory way. Noise of this sort can also be controlled by the way in which you implement pedagogical strategies to control it. However, as we examined previously, there is a certain extent to which the acoustical properties of a classroom impact on the noise level within a room. Clearly, satisfactory acoustical conditions should be a prerequisite for classroom teaching and the room acoustics should not work against the teaching activities that you want your students to engage with. One of the most important aspects in this respect is to minimise the amount of reflected sound within the classroom. Reflected sound will mask the sound of your voice and will impair the students' ability to hear you clearly. Consequently, you will have to speak louder in order to be heard and, if the reflective surfaces remain in place, that amount of reflected sound will also increase; a vicious circle that has very negative consequences for you, your vocal health and, as we will see, your own wellbeing.

That said, the researchers also cite what is known as the 'Lombard effect'. This was first noted in 1909 by Étienne Lombard, a French otolaryngologist, who discovered that speakers tended to increase their vocal effort when speaking in a space with loud background noise in order to enhance their audibility. This change in voice did not only include a change in loudness, but also meant that other acoustic features such a pitch, the speed of vocal delivery and the duration of specific syllables were all altered. This meant that the speaker's ability to be heard within the noisy environment increased.

The Rantala study also presents an interesting historical reflection on the level of classroom and ambient noise in the school environment. As we discussed above, ambient noise levels in the schools surveyed were within the recommended levels; activity noise levels were in line with research undertaken in previous decades (Rantala et al. 2015, p. 1401). In terms of the vocal delivery by the studied teachers, the researchers found that ambient and activity noise affected their vocal performance in different ways. As might have been predicted, when faced with ambient noise, teachers raised their voices. However, when faced with louder activity noise teachers' voices increased in volume but changed less in terms of other vocal elements. The Lombard effect seemed to influence teachers' voices more consistently under ambient noise rather than activity noise. The researchers continue:

> Some of the characteristics of ambient noise may account for speakers' reactions to it. A typical feature of such noise is that it is mostly constant and continuous. In ambient noise, speakers to not have the same avoidance opportunities they have if the noise fluctuates, as is the case with activity noise. Under fluctuating noise, people are prone to decrease speech in nosy moments but increase it in silent ones. The other common feature for ambient noise is that it contains low frequencies. Consequently, people commonly find ambient noise to be louder than one could conclude on the basis of the values of a sound level meter alone. In addition, low-frequency noise has been found to be annoying, and this effect persists even after the apparent loudness has decreased. Annoyance, in turn, raise stress and this affects voice production.
>
> (Rantala et al. 2015, p. 1402)

The researchers in the Kristiansen study (Kristiansen et al. 2014) also noted the more negative features associated with having to contend with noisy classroom environments. They noted that increased noise levels and enhanced vocal load led to teachers feeling more fatigue and stressed after a day's work. They also found evidence that teachers had lower energy, performed more poorly in cognitive tasks and had an increase in vocal symptoms during the day:

> The reduction in percentage of correct responses in the cognitive test TBT correlated significantly with the teachers' average vocal load during the day. There was also a correlation with noise exposure in the expected direction, but this effect was just above the level of statistical significance. The reason that vocal load correlated stronger with cognitive fatigue measures could be that an increased vocal load during the day is better indicator for the mental workload than the background noise level itself. For example, when interviewed about noise, teachers have told us that they do not always feel challenged by a high level of classroom noise because high noise levels indicate active participation by the pupils in the teaching. It is only when it obstructs the teaching that noise becomes a problem. Speculatively, a raised vocal load may reflect situations where noise has become an obstruction to teaching.
>
> (ibid., pp. 858–859)

As we have said throughout this chapter so far, the noise level in the classroom itself is not the issue here. When that noise level 'obstructs' the ability to communicate clearly through vocal delivery, then problems begin to occur. This was also a feature of the Rantala study. The 'activity noise', i.e. the sound of students' working, seemed to impact less on teachers' vocal delivery. They state:

> Activity noise usually comprises frequencies similar to those of the human voice and so largely masks speech. Speakers are prone to compensate for this by increasing prosody – that is, not linearly raising the pitch and loudness but varying the levels of these vocal features.
>
> (Rantala et al. 2015, p. 1402)

The researchers noted another key recommendation of our book, which is that using a wide range of approaches to communicate in the classroom does not depend on your voice alone. They write:

> Teachers often report that they have developed strategies to use if pupils' classroom work turns noisy: Instead of shouting over the racket, they wait until the noise abates or they use other means to get attention, such as clapping their hands, using a whistle, or giving orders with the help of pictures.
>
> (Rantala et al. 2015, p. 1402)

Quite so. Finding a rich and varied pedagogical approach is a key aspect of effective communication in the classroom. We have noticed teachers using a range of techniques to gain the attention of a class without raising their voice. Why don't you try the following:

1. Putting your hand in the air and asking students to do the same. Tell them that they have to be silent when their hand is in the air. It takes a bit of practice but it can work really well.

2. Turning the lights in the room off and on to signal that you want everyone to stop what they are doing and pay attention on you. It's a bit Pavlovian but it works!

3. Using a whistle! This is a favourite of PE teachers for a reason. However, there is no reason why it shouldn't work in an internal space too. As a contrary approach, we knew a teacher who had a small gong that had a very beautiful but quite distinctive sound. It was loud or shouty (like a whistle) but had a sonorous, deep tone that really cut through classroom noise effectively. It was certainly a little more civilised than a whistle and perhaps more suitable for indoor use.

4. Clapping a catchy rhythm (think something like a football chant) and teach the students a short response. This can work as an aural cue. Having performed the question (you) and the answer (them) the rule is that they have to stop talking and listen to you.

Whatever technique you use, and there are loads of others that you'll see being used by teachers day in day out, the important thing is that you are not using your voice for crowd control! Over time, this can really help you preserve your voice and its vocal quality, allowing you to use it in the right way and for the most productive purposes. Additionally, techniques like these will also help you avoid stress, tiredness and cognitive overload. Basically, you'll perform better as a teacher!

Amplifying your voice

Many of the research studies that we have considered in this chapter have suggested that finding ways to amplify your voice could be a beneficial strategy and help you preserve good vocal delivery and vocal health over a long teaching career. This is not something that is routinely done in schools within the United Kingdom and we have to wonder, given the almost overall consensus in the literature that this would be a good thing, why this has not happened. We suspect that the main reason comes down to cost. But, that said, we should also take into account the cost to schools (and, ultimately, the Government) of enforced absences through illness, tiredness and stress associated with the demands of teaching, many of which are related to the stresses and strains of vocal delivery in poor acoustic and physical environments. However, this is not a problem we are going to solve here!

So, what can we advise? First, if you are lucky to be in a space that has a fixed form of voice amplification or reinforcement then please use it! We know that many people find it a little odd to use a microphone and that they can appear a bit self-conscious to start with. You need to get over this quickly. Practise beforehand and think about learning a little microphone technique. In summary, if the microphone is too close you will get:

■ Popping from consonant sounds like B and P;

■ Wind noise caused by breath;

■ An over-emphasised bass due to proximity;

■ The possibility of the microphone hitting teeth or lips.

If the microphone is too far away:

■ The weak signal makes background noise more noticeable;

■ You will get unclear sound and too much hiss on playback.

With the microphone correctly placed you will get a strong signal with little risk of external noise and, most importantly, your voice will be amplified without any risk of vocal strain.

If you are not in a classroom with a PA system, there are still some other options for you to consider. The wireless solutions for microphones have moved on significantly in recent years and there are products available today that link wireless functionality with USB connections. So, if you have access to computer and speakers you could consider using those to help amplify your voice within the classroom. Products such as Samson's XPD1 lavalier wireless digital microphone systems link the lavalier microphone (a small, indiscreet microphone that can clip on your shirt or blouse) wirelessly to a USB port that plugs into your computer. This is meant for recording purposes but if you send the input of the microphone to the output of the computer speakers (or whatever monitors etc. might be attached to the computer) then you have created a simple PA system using the components that you have to hand and for minimum expense.

If the wireless option doesn't seem appropriate for your classroom (or you don't have a computer or monitor speakers), then a straightforward wired dynamic microphone like the Samson Q7 (around £30) or the Rode M1 (around £70) can be connected to a portable desktop monitor/amplifier like the Roland Cube Lite (around £120). Although systems like this will only send out between 10 and 20 W of volume, this is more than enough for spoken work within the classroom and will certainly ease the strain on your voice.

Amplifying your voice might seem like quite an extreme step for teachers who are used to projecting their voice in the classroom. But, as we have seen, the risks to teachers' vocal health over the medium to long term are significant. Anything that you can do to restrict the harmful effects of straining your voice is surely worth considering.

Remember that although your voice is an important tool it is not the only one that you have. Good teachers rest their voices whenever possible and use a range of non-verbal signs to ensure that their students remain focussed and engaged. If you are really struggling with your voice, the best solution is to take some time off work and recover fully. Just ploughing on teaching and speaking with a damaged voice risks permanent vocal damage, which must be avoided at all costs.

And, finally, 'a good night's sleep is an essential factor for appropriate vocal production' (Ferreira et al. 2010, p. 86), so, onto our final section.

Time for a nap!

Congratulations on reaching the final few pages of our book! We think that all your hard work in engaging with our thoughts on how to use your voice productively in the classroom should result in a reward. Yes, it's time for a short power nap! Here's our justification for your reward (please read it before you nod off!).

We know that the sleep habits of young people can come into conflict with the times that school operates:

> Early morning school schedules are in the opposite direction to the sleep–wake cycle in adolescence and early adulthood. This conflict leads to sleep deprivation and irregular patterns.
>
> (Azevedo et al. 2008, p. 34)

This offers a biological explanation as to why some of your students may not seem at their best first thing in the morning. We also know that teaching is a high-stress occupation:

> HSE [Health and Safety Executive] research in 2000 found teaching to be the most stressful profession in the UK, with 41.5% of teachers reporting themselves as 'highly stressed'. For comparison, the incidence of any kind of stress across the working population is believed to be less than 20 per cent.
>
> From 2003 to 2006 statistics show that the highest reported rates of occupational stress, depression or anxiety were to be found in the teaching and research professions – indeed the levels of stress amongst teachers were twice that for 'all occupations'.
>
> (NUT 2008)

We also know that 'levels of stress among teachers in the UK compare unfavourably with their European peers' (NASUWT 2012). Teaching in the UK is a high-risk occupation in terms of stress!

Dealing with stress is only one aspect of the job, though. Simply being in front of a class is tiring, and as good teachers spend very little of their time sitting down whilst teaching (at least, this is our assertion and hopefully you'll agree that it is better to be standing up and mobile most of the time in the classroom), there are physical as well as mental demands. From everything that we have discussed in this book, we know that the demands on your voice are significant and that there are real dangers of taking these for granted. We have saved this exploration of potential risks to our final chapter because it is important. You need to think very carefully about how to protect your voice in the short, medium and long term.

We know from many anecdotal accounts that one of the first things that many teachers do when getting home is to have a short sleep. Research has shown that this is actually beneficial: 'Short daytime naps of less than 30 minutes have been shown to have positive effects on daytime alertness' (Hayashi et al. 2005, p. 829). This is good news for all those people who have been feeling guilty about dozing off before beginning an evening's marking!

We also know from our experiences in leading PGCE and other teacher training routes that students find their time in school one of the most demanding things they have done, and that it has serious effect on their sleep patterns. Those at university find that this has an effect upon their lifestyles, and that teacher training students prefer to flat-share together, so that their colleagues, even if at different stages in their courses, fully appreciate that those on placement will need early nights, and will not appreciate late-night parties!

Trying to teach when tired is difficult, and full alertness is needed, so sleep really is an important factor that teachers need to consider. And if nagged by non-teacher friends to go out, it can be helpful to say that your job is more stressful than theirs, and there are statistics to prove it!

This is the final paragraph in our book. So, before sign off, can we say 'Thank You!' for getting to the end of the final sentences. You deserve the chance to go and have a legitimate nap for a few minutes. Good luck in your teaching career. We trust that you have found at least a few useful things in this book that will help you on your teaching journey.

References

Arboleda, B. & Frederick, A. (2006) 'Considerations for maintenance of postural alignment for voice production'. *Journal of Voice* 22:1, 90–99. Also available from: http://www. claudiafriedlander.com/Postural%20Alignment%20for%20Voice%20Production.pdf [last accessed 6/3/17].

Awan, S. N. (2013) 'Both direct and indirect behavioral treatments are beneficial for the treatment of voice disorders in teachers'. *Evidence-Based Communication Assessment and Intervention* 7:2, 57–62, DOI: 10.1080/17489539.2013.846609.

Azevedo, C. V. M., Sousa, I., Paul, K., MacLeish, M. Y., Mondejar, M. T., Sarabia, J. A., Ángeles Rol, M. & Madrid, J. A. (2008) 'Teaching chronobiology and sleep habits in school and university'. *Mind, Brain, and Education* 2:1, 34–47.

Clausen, T., Kristiansen, J., Hansen J., Pejtersen, J. & Burr, H. (2013) 'Exposure to disturbing noise and risk of long-term sickness absence among office workers: A prospective analysis of register-based outcomes'. *International Archives of Occupational and Environmental Health* 86:7, 729–734.

Cutiva, C., Vogel, I. & Burdorf, A. (2013) 'Voice disorders in teachers and their associations with work-related factors: A systematic review'. *Journal of Communication Disorders* 46, 143–155.

Ferreira, L. P., de Oliveira Latorre, M. R. D., Pinto Giannini, S. P., de Assis Moura Ghirardi, A. C., de Fraga e Karmann, D., Silva, E. E. & Figueira, S. (2010) 'Influence of abusive vocal habits, hydration, mastication, and sleep in the occurrence of vocal symptoms in teachers'. *Journal of Voice* 24:1, 86–92.

Hayashi, M., Motoyoshi, N. & Hori, T. (2005) 'Recuperative power of a short daytime nap with or without stage 2 sleep'. *Sleep* 28:7, 829–36.

Hunter, E. & Titze, I. (2010) 'Variations in intensity, fundamental frequency, and voicing for teachers in occupational versus nonoccupational settings'. *Journal of Speech, Language and Hearing Research* 53, 862–875.

Kooijman, P., de Jong, F., Oudes M., Huinck, W., van Acht H. & Graamans, K. (2005) 'Muscular tension and body posture in relation to voice handicap and voice quality in teachers with persistent voice complaints'. *Folia Phoniatrica et Logopaedica* 57, 134–147.

Kristiansen, J. (2010) 'Is noise exposure in non-industrial work environments associated with increased sickness absence?' *Noise and Vibration Worldwide* 4:5, 9–16.

Kristiansen, J., Lund, S., Persson, R., Shibuya, H., Nielsen, P & Scholz, M. (2014) 'A study of classroom acoustics and school teachers' noise exposure, voice load and speaking time during teaching, and the effects on vocal and mental fatigue development'. *International Archives of Occupational and Environmental Health* 87:8, 851–860.

Laukkanen, A. & Kankare, E. (2006) 'Vocal loading related changes in male teachers' voices investigated before and after a working day'. *Folia Phoniatrica et Logopaedica* 58, 229–239.

Laukkanen, A., Ilomäki I., Leppänen K. & Vilkman E. (2008) 'Acoustic measures and self-reports of vocal fatigue by female teachers'. *Journal of Voice*, 22, 283–289.

Masuda, T., Ikeda, Y., Manako, H. & Komiyama, S. (1993) 'Analysis of vocal abuse: Fluctuations in phonation time and intensity in 4 groups of speakers'. *Acta Otolaryngol* 113, 547–552.

Mendell, M., Mirer, A., Cheung, K., Tong, M. & Douwes, J. (2011) 'Respiratory and allergic health effects of dampness, mold, and dampness-related agents: A review of the epidemiologic evidence'. *Environmental Health Perspectives* 119, 748–756.

NASUWT (2012) 'European survey reveals UK teachers suffer more stress than European counterparts'. http://www.nasuwt.org.uk/MemberSupport/MemberGroups/Bulletins/ETUCSurvey/NASUWT_009159 [last accessed 18/3/17].

NUT (2008) 'Tackling teacher stress'. http://www.teachers.org.uk/stress [last accessed 18/3/17].

Paris, M. (2007) 'Terry Wogan and Ken Bruce are beloved because they soar above English ideas of class'. https://www.spectator.co.uk/2007/06/terry-wogan-and-ken-bruce-are-beloved-because-they-soar-above-english-ideas-of-class/# [last accessed 29/3/17].

Puglisi, G., Cantor Cutiva, L., Pavese, L., Castellana, A., Bona, M., Fasolis, S., Lorenzatti, V., Carullo, A., Burdorf, A., Bronuzzi, F. & Astolfi, A. (2015) 'Acoustic comfort in high-school classrooms for students and teachers'. Sixth International Building Physics Conference, IBPC.

Rantala, L., Hakala, S., Holmqvist, S. & Sala, E. (2013) 'Connections between voice ergonomic risk factors in classrooms and teachers' voice production'. *Folia Phoniatrica et Logopaedica* 64, 278–282.

Rantala, L., Hakala, S., Holmqvist, S. & Sala, E. (2015) 'Classroom noise and teachers' voice production'. *Journal of Speech, Language and Hearing Research* 58, 1397–1406.

Roy, N., Merrill, R., Thibeault, S., Parsa, R., Gray, S. & Smith, E. (2004) 'Prevalence of voice disorders in teachers and the general population'. *Journal of Speech, Language and Hearing Research* 47, 281–293.

Rubin, J., Blake E. & Mathieson, L. (2007) 'Musculoskeletal patterns in patients with voice disorders'. *Journal of Voice* 21, 477–484.

Sala, E., Hytönen, M., Tupasela, O. & Estlander, T. (1996) 'Occupational laryngitis with immediate allergy or immediate type specific chemical hypersensitivity'. *Clinical Otolaryngology* 21, 42–48.

Shield, B. & Dockrell, J. (2003) 'The effects of noise on children at school: A review'. *Building Acoustics* 10:2, 97–106.

Shield, B. & Dockrell, J. (2004) 'External and internal noise surveys of London primary schools'. *The Journal of the Acoustical Society of America* 115:2, 730–738.

Sihvo, M. (1997) 'Voice in test: studies on sound level measurement and on the effects of various combinations of environmental humidity, speaking output level and body posture on voice range profiles' (dissertation). Tampere, University of Tampere.

Simberg, S., Sala, E., Tuomainen, J. & Rönnemaa, A. (2009) 'Vocal symptoms and allergy: A pilot study'. *Journal of Voice* 23, 136–139.

Szymanowski, A., Borst, K. & Sataloff, R. (2014) 'Voice disorders in teachers: Examining the problem and evaluating prevention'. *Journal of Singing* 71:2, 201–206.

Titze, R., Lemke, J., & Montequin, D. (1997) 'Populations in the U.S. workforce who rely on voice as a primary tool of trade: A preliminary report'. *Journal of Voice* 11, 254–259.

Titze I., Hunter E. & Svec, J. (2007) 'Voicing and silence periods in daily and weekly vocalizations of teachers'. *The Journal of the Acoustic Society of America* 121, 469–478.

Wilson Arboleda B. & Frederick A. (2008) 'Considerations for maintenance of postural alignment for voice production'. *Journal of Voice* 22, 90–99.

Witt, R., Taylor, L., Regner, M. & Jiang, J. (2011) 'Effects of surface dehydration on mucosal wave amplitude and frequency in excised canine larynges'. *Otolaryngol – Head and Neck Surgery* 144, 108–113.

Index

Made in the USA
Las Vegas, NV
28 March 2022

46457796R00096